More Praise for
Healing the Heart of Democracy

"In Selma, Alabama, on 'Bloody Sunday' in 1965, we were beaten at the Edmund Pettus Bridge. A few days later, we marched all the way to Montgomery. A few months after that, President Lyndon Johnson signed the Voting Rights Act. When we set out to cross that bridge, we wanted to bridge the divide of racial discrimination. The burden of race was too heavy; we wanted our country to lay it down. We Americans have been trying to bridge the great divides in this great country for a long time. In this book, Parker J. Palmer urges us to 'keep on walking, keep on talking'—just as we did in the civil rights movement—until we cross those bridges together." —**Congressman John Lewis**, recipient of the Martin Luther King Jr. Nonviolent Peace Prize and the Presidential Medal of Freedom and coauthor of *Walking with the Wind*

"*Healing the Heart of Democracy* by Parker J. Palmer is a book born for this moment. Wise, evocative, and pragmatic at its core, this dream for a new politics is grounded in dignity and liberty for all. In this time of civic rupture and discord, I wish this book could be placed in the hands of every member of Congress, every governor, mayor, and state legislator in America. May these words spark a new conversation within our communities, focusing on what binds us together rather than what tears us apart. And may we see this challenge to engage fully within public life not only as a calling, but as a personal commitment to our own ethical stance toward life. This is a book that calls forth our highest selves in the name of a spiritual democracy." —**Terry Tempest Williams**, author of *The Open Space of Democracy*

"It is hard to imagine a single moment in American history when this book's wisdom would not have been invaluable, but it is even harder to imagine a time when such wisdom is more desperately needed than right now. Parker J. Palmer's unblinking gaze into the habits of the human heart, beginning with his own deeply personal introspection, yields the most important manifesto in generations for breaking through the divisiveness that has paralyzed our democracy to the point of making it almost unrecognizable. Palmer manages to share the most profound insights about our history, culture, and current developments, yet in the refreshingly readable tone of a caring neighbor who has kept a watchful eye on your house when you were away longer than expected. In its compassion, tolerance, prescription, and urgency, this book stands alone as a beacon showing what may well be the only tenable path forward for our nation in a perilous time." —**Bill Shore**, founder of Share Our Strength and author of *The Cathedral Within* and *The Imaginations of Unreasonable Men*

"Parker J. Palmer's newest book is his most ambitious. Personal and prophetic, it blends heartache and hope, encouraging us to bring 'chutzpah and humility' to our public lives. The book awakens the open mind and open heart Palmer sees as essential to a flourishing democracy. No matter what our political leanings, all who harbor concerns about the quality of public discourse and decision making in twenty-first-century America will find here a wise and kindred spirit who reminds us of choices we can be making now to help 'reweave the tattered fabric of our civic life.' At stake is our common future and the vitality of the fragile democracy we inherited and neglect at our peril. If you find yourself feeling at times that nothing you do will matter, you will close this book appreciating how much you can do, and how much depends on you." —**Diana Chapman Walsh**, President Emerita of Wellesley College

"This book is a gracefully written anthem to democracy. Not just the democracy of the vote, but a larger conception of the democracy of how we live together across all that divides us. *Healing the Heart of Democracy* breaks new ground in marrying the individual capacity of the human heart, broken though it must become, with the irresolvable tensions inherent in the institutions, politics, and aspirations of a nation. Democracy here is as much the will to welcome a stranger across the tracks as it is to reconcile very different ideas about what is good for a people. It makes democracy personal as well as political. Palmer also breathes new life into what it means to be a citizen—accountable, compassionate, fiercely realistic. The book is a political and personal imperative, reminding us of our covenant with the larger community of souls. The author has been the prophet to many for decades and *Healing the Heart of Democracy* will only deepen that gift and bring it out into new corners of this troubled world." —**Peter Block** and **John McKnight**, coauthors of *The Abundant Community: Awakening the Power of Families and Neighborhoods*

"In this book, Parker J. Palmer brings together the wisdom of a lifetime. There is no one better suited than Palmer to illuminate that place where 'all of the ways of our knowing' converge, and to bring it to our common attention at this exquisitely heartbreaking and promising moment. This is the manual we need for refashioning our life together—for recovering the heart, the very core, of our selves and our democracy." —**Krista Tippett**, journalist, host of American Public Media's Being, and author of *Speaking of Faith* and *Einstein's God*

"This book could not be more timely and needed in our country today. Parker J. Palmer gives voice to the yearning for democracy and a politics that honors the human spirit. As one who has been guided through a time of personal reflection with Parker, I invite you to join in a journey through these chapters. He examines the courage required to hold life's tensions consciously and faithfully—and perhaps, as our hearts break open, find ourselves standing and acting creatively 'in the gap.'" —**Congresswoman Lois Capps**, grandmother, mother, nurse, and seeker after democracy

"*Healing the Heart of Democracy* is a courageous work that is honest and true, human and humble, glitteringly intelligent and unabashedly hopeful. Parker J. Palmer has beautifully articulated our collective

longing for constructive political conversation that holds the tensions of the democratic process creatively and respectfully. Here is a clear-eyed assessment of the pressing needs we face in our country and our world, framed by a conviction that we have the means within us and within our communities to meet the challenge. Palmer gives us constructive language, historical context, and a practical vision for how we as individuals and communities can get to the real heart of the matter."
—**Carrie Newcomer**, activist and singer-songwriter, *The Geography of Light* and *Before and After*

"In *Healing the Heart of Democracy*, Parker J. Palmer brings his extraordinary vision and experience to bear on the widening divisions in our culture. Regardless of your political persuasion, this book is a sorely needed medicine in how we meet each other, listen to each other, and care for each other. This is a master work by a master: a clear and uplifting resource that keeps shining light in all the dark places. Chapter IV alone would help anyone rebuild a city. Like Socrates and Thoreau, Palmer is that rare, deep seer who is at home in the streets; an inner everyman who keeps speaking from a mind descended into the heart; a teacher by example who has the courage to stand openly and honestly in the public square." —**Mark Nepo**, author of *The Book of Awakening* and *As Far as the Heart Can See*

"Parker J. Palmer writes, 'The heart of the world itself has an unwritten history.' That was true until now. In this brave and visionary book, Palmer re-imagines our political lives, not as partisan shouting matches among a homogenous and disconnected elite, but as a deeply personal process within which all Americans—especially those of us inheriting this broken polity—have a chance to be heard, heal, and get on with the eternal work of perfecting this nation. As he recasts 'the political,' even the most frustrated and cynical among us are moved to 'stand in the tragic gap' with a renewed sense of our own quiet power."
—**Courtney E. Martin**, author of *Do It Anyway: The New Generation of Activists*

"This book is a 'must read' for everyone who is concerned about the state of our democracy and has ever despaired about what can be done. As you take in Parker J. Palmer's stories and plainspoken analysis, you will look at yourself and others in a different light; his penetrating insights will inspire you to claim your full human capacities and to take part in healing democracy 'from the inside out.'" —**Martha L. McCoy**, executive director of Everyday Democracy

"Reflecting on the words of Parker J. Palmer in *Healing the Heart of Democracy*, I am convinced that all of us—as citizens and as elected officials—can learn to bridge the divides that keep us from genuinely respecting one another. In my own reflections on the meaning of democracy, I find encouragement in this inspirational book. Becoming good stewards of our democracy means having a commitment to our collective well-being, rather than each struggling to get his or her own. We must care about the common good, which means working for the many, not just the privileged few. Parker, through sharing his own life's struggles, reveals the common struggles we all endure in life. He also provides us with a way forward—a way forward with hope."
—**Congresswoman Tammy Baldwin**

"Parker J. Palmer has been our mentor as we've weathered the rough and tumble of political life. His work guides us again and again to seek grounding in the courage to embrace our own deepest questions. Now, in this compelling new book, he turns his unsparing insights to our wounded democracy. Palmer reminds us that democracy depends on citizens who not only engage with the political process but also engage with each other. He challenges us to recognize that a more vital democracy begins within each of us, as we learn to hold the tensions inherent in community life and no longer fear to tread that most difficult terrain—the broken places in our own hearts." —**Kathy Gille** served for twenty years as a senior congressional aide. **Doug Tanner**, her husband, is a founder and former president of The Faith and Politics Institute.

"This is an inspiring book, one that should be read and talked about in every family, book club, classroom, boardroom, congregation, and hall of government in our country. Parker J. Palmer writes with clarity, good sense, balance, honesty, humor, and humility, focusing on the essence of what is needed from each of us for the survival of our democracy."
—**Thomas F. Beech**, president emeritus, The Fetzer Institute

Healing
THE *Heart* OF
Democracy

Other Books by Parker J. Palmer

A Hidden Wholeness
Let Your Life Speak
The Courage to Teach
The Active Life
To Know as We Are Known
The Company of Strangers
The Promise of Paradox
The Heart of Higher Education
(with Arthur Zajonc and Megan Scribner)

Healing
THE *Heart* OF
Democracy

THE COURAGE TO
CREATE A POLITICS WORTHY
OF THE HUMAN SPIRIT

Parker J. PALMER

JOSSEY-BASS
A Wiley Imprint
www.josseybass.com

Copyright © 2011 by Parker J. Palmer. All rights reserved.

Published by Jossey-Bass
A Wiley Imprint
989 Market Street, San Francisco, CA 94103-1741—www.josseybass.com

No part of this publication may be reproduced, stored in a retrieval system, or transmitted in any form or by any means, electronic, mechanical, photocopying, recording, scanning, or otherwise, except as permitted under Section 107 or 108 of the 1976 United States Copyright Act, without either the prior written permission of the publisher, or authorization through payment of the appropriate per-copy fee to the Copyright Clearance Center, Inc., 222 Rosewood Drive, Danvers, MA 01923, 978-750-8400, fax 978-646-8600, or on the Web at www.copyright.com. Requests to the publisher for permission should be addressed to the Permissions Department, John Wiley & Sons, Inc., 111 River Street, Hoboken, NJ 07030, 201-748-6011, fax 201-748-6008, or online at www.wiley.com/go/permissions.

Additional credit lines are listed on page 236.

Readers should be aware that Internet Web sites offered as citations and/or sources for further information may have changed or disappeared between the time this was written and when it is read.

Limit of Liability/Disclaimer of Warranty: While the publisher and author have used their best efforts in preparing this book, they make no representations or warranties with respect to the accuracy or completeness of the contents of this book and specifically disclaim any implied warranties of merchantability or fitness for a particular purpose. No warranty may be created or extended by sales representatives or written sales materials. The advice and strategies contained herein may not be suitable for your situation. You should consult with a professional where appropriate. Neither the publisher nor author shall be liable for any loss of profit or any other commercial damages, including but not limited to special, incidental, consequential, or other damages.

Jossey-Bass books and products are available through most bookstores. To contact Jossey-Bass directly call our Customer Care Department within the U.S. at 800-956-7739, outside the U.S. at 317-572-3986, or fax 317-572-4002.

Jossey-Bass also publishes its books in a variety of electronic formats. Some content that appears in print may not be available in electronic books.

Library of Congress Cataloging-in-Publication Data

Palmer, Parker J.
  Healing the heart of democracy : the courage to create a politics worthy of the human spirit / Parker J. Palmer.
       p. cm.
    Includes index.
    ISBN 978-0-470-59080-5 (hardback); 978-1-118-08448-9 (ebk); 978-1-118-08449-6 (ebk); 978-1-118-08450-2 (ebk)
    1. Citizenship—United States. 2. Political participation—United States. 3. Civics. I. Title.
    JK1759.P33 2011
    320.973—dc22

                                                                                    2011014366

Printed in the United States of America
FIRST EDITION
HB Printing   10   9   8   7   6   5   4   3   2   1

[CONTENTS]

In memory of

Christina Taylor Green (2001–2011)
Addie Mae Collins (1949–1963)
Denise McNair (1951–1963)
Carole Robertson (1949–1963)
Cynthia Wesley (1949–1963)

Christina died when an assassin in Tucson, Arizona, opened fire at a public event hosted by Congresswoman Gabrielle Giffords, who was seriously wounded. Addie Mae, Denise, Carole, and Cynthia died when violent racists bombed the 16th Street Baptist Church in Birmingham, Alabama.

When we forget that politics is about weaving a fabric of compassion and justice on which everyone can depend, the first to suffer are the most vulnerable among us—our children, the elderly, the mentally ill, the poor, and the homeless. As they suffer, so does the integrity of our democracy.

May the heartbreaking deaths of these children—and the hope and promise that was in their young lives—help us find the courage to create a politics worthy of the human spirit.

The human heart is the first home of democracy. It is where we embrace our questions. Can we be equitable? Can we be generous? Can we listen with our whole beings, not just our minds, and offer our attention rather than our opinions? And do we have enough resolve in our hearts to act courageously, relentlessly, without giving up—ever—trusting our fellow citizens to join with us in our determined pursuit of a living democracy?

—Terry Tempest Williams, "Engagement"[1]

The Politics of the Brokenhearted

In a dark time, the eye begins to see.

—THEODORE ROETHKE, "In a Dark Time"[1]

I began this book in a season of heartbreak—personal and political heartbreak—that soon descended into a dark night of the soul. It took months to find my way back to the light and six years to complete the book. But as I fumbled in the dark, the poet Roethke's words proved true time and again: my eyes were opened to new insights, and my heart was opened to new life. The evidence will, I hope, come clear as this book unfolds.

In 2004, I turned sixty-five. As I entered my "golden years" and saw how much of that gold was rust, I found myself disheartened by the diminishments that come with age. Family members and friends were failing and dying. Visions I once held for my life were slipping beyond my reach. My body kept reminding me that I am just a tad more mortal than I had imagined I would be. And I was no longer able to "read" American culture as easily as I could when my generation was helping to author it. It was as if I had lost the secret decoder ring I owned when I was a kid, and with it my ability to make sense of twenty-first-century life.

As the shape of my personal life became less familiar and sometimes more frightening, the same thing was happening in American politics as viewed from my vantage point. Dismayed by the state of the nation,

1

I began to feel like a displaced person in my own land. The terrorist attacks of September 11, 2001, had deepened America's appreciation of democracy *and* activated demons that threaten it, demons still at large today. Wounded and overwhelmed by fear, we soon went to war against a country that had no direct connection to the attacks. Many Americans seemed willing to abandon their constitutional rights along with our international treaty obligations.[2] Some Americans, including elected officials, were quick to accuse protesters and dissenters of being unpatriotic or worse, fragmenting the civic community on which democracy depends.

I am no stranger to this democracy's moments of peril, which have been precipitated by Democrats and Republicans alike. I lived through McCarthy's communist witch hunts; the pushback to the civil rights movement; the political assassinations of the 1960s; the burning of our cities; Vietnam, the Pentagon Papers, Watergate; and the electoral debacle of 2000. I have witnessed the rapid erosion of the middle class and the growing power of big money, an oligarchy of wealth, to trump the will of the people. But with fear and fragmentation becoming staples of our national life, and with the haunting sense that our "booming economy" was likely to implode, democracy felt even more imperiled to me in the America of 2004.

As our distrust of "the other" beyond our borders hardened and we began making aliens of each other (a "we" that included me), I fell into a spiral of outrage and despair. How did we forget that our differences are among our most valuable assets? What happened to "we have nothing to fear but fear itself"? When will we learn that violence in the long run creates at least as many problems as it solves? Why do we not value life, every life, no matter whose or where? Or understand that the measure of national greatness is not only how successful the strong can be but how well we support the weak?

And where have "We the People" gone—we who have the power to reclaim democracy for its highest purposes, unless we allow ourselves to be divided and conquered by the enemy within and among us?

∞

When things we care about fall apart, heartbreak happens. In my sixty-fifth year, it was happening, again, to me.[3] I soon began to realize that this episode was darker than most of those I had known before: I was descending into depression, my third time down as an adult. Clearly I am predisposed to this form of mental anguish, so I cannot claim that heartbreak was the sole source of my misery. But neither can I attribute the whole of this episode to brain chemistry or genetics. There are times when the heart, like the canary in the coal mine, breathes in the world's toxicity and begins to die.

Much has been said about the "voice of depression." It is a voice that speaks despairingly about the whole of one's life no matter how good parts of it may be—a voice so loud and insistent that when it speaks, it is the only sound one can hear. I know that voice well. I have spent long days and nights listening to its deadly urgings.

Less has been said about the life-giving fact that, as poet Theodore Roethke writes, "In a dark time, the eye begins to see." During my sojourn on the dark side, it was hard to believe that my vision was growing sharper or to make sense of what I was seeing. And yet as I slowly came back to life, I found that I had gained new clarity about myself, the community I depend on, and my call to reengage with its politics and relearn how to hold its tensions in a life-giving way.

During my recovery, I discovered a book that helped me understand how heartbreak and depression—two of the most isolating and disabling experiences I know—can expand one's sense of connectedness and evoke the heart's capacity to employ tension in the service of life. *Lincoln's Melancholy,* by Joshua Shenk, is a probing examination of our sixteenth president's journey with depression.[4] What was then called "melancholy" first appeared in Lincoln's twenties, when neighbors occasionally took him in for fear he might take his own life. Lincoln struggled with this affliction until the day he died, a dark thread laced through a life driven by the conviction that he was born to render some sort of public service.

Lincoln's need to preserve his life by embracing and integrating his own darkness and light made him uniquely qualified to help America preserve the Union. Because he knew dark and light intimately—knew them as inseparable elements of everything human—he refused to split North and South into "good guys" and "bad guys," a split that might have taken us closer to the national version of suicide.

Instead, in his second inaugural address, delivered on March 4, 1865, a month before the end of the Civil War, Lincoln appealed for "malice toward none" and "charity for all," animated by what one writer calls an "awe-inspiring sense of love for *all*" who bore the brunt of the battle.[5] In his appeal to a deeply divided America, Lincoln points to an essential fact of our life together: if we are to survive and thrive, we must hold its divisions and contradictions with compassion, lest we lose our democracy.

Lincoln has much to teach us about embracing political tension in a way that opens our hearts to each other, no matter how deep our differences. That way begins "in here" as we work on reconciling whatever divides us from ourselves—and then moves out with healing power into a world of many divides, drawing light out of darkness, community out of chaos, and life out of death.

In my experience, the best therapy for personal problems comes from reaching out as well as looking in. Reading about Lincoln as my healing continued, I began to wonder about my own ability to reach across the divides that threaten our Union today, not as an elected leader but as a citizen, a trust holder of democracy. To make this something other than a pious exercise in forced altruism—which always leads me to feel-good failures that end in a pathetic "God knows I tried!"—I needed to find a true point of identity with people whose basic beliefs are contrary to mine.

What do I have in common with people who, for example, regard their religious or political convictions as so authoritative that they feel no need to listen to anyone who sees things differently—especially that small subgroup of extremists who would use violence to advance their views? My own experience of political heartbreak gave me a clue. Perhaps we share an abiding grief over some of modernity's worst features: its mindless relativism, corrosive cynicism, disdain for tradition and human dignity, indifference to suffering and death.

How shall we respond to these cultural trends that diminish all of us? On this question, I, too, have a nonnegotiable conviction: violence can never be the answer. Instead, we must protect people's freedom to believe and behave as they will, within the rule of law; assent to majority rule while dedicating ourselves to protecting minority rights; embrace and act on our responsibility to care for one another; seek to educate ourselves about our critical differences; come together in dialogue toward mutual understanding; and speak without fear against all that diminishes us, including the use of violence.

With people who are irrevocably committed to violence, I may never find the smallest patch of common ground. Could I find one with others whose views differ sharply from mine—a small patch, perhaps, but one large enough that we could stand there and talk for a while? I had reason to believe that the answer might be yes. For example, I know of daylong dialogue programs for people who differ on difficult issues like abortion where participants are forbidden from proclaiming their positions on the issue until the last hour of the day. Instead, they are coached in the art of personal storytelling and then invited to share the experiences that gave rise to their beliefs while others *simply listen.*

Hearing each other's stories, which are often stories of heartbreak, can create an unexpected bond between so-called pro-life and pro-choice people. When two people discover that parallel experiences led them to contrary conclusions, they are more likely to hold their differences respectfully, knowing that they have experienced similar forms of grief.[6] The more you know about another person's story, the less possible it is to see that person as your enemy.

Abortion is one of the many issues that generate what some people have called the "politics of rage." And yet rage is simply one of the masks that heartbreak wears. When we share the sources of our pain with each other instead of hurling our convictions like rocks at "enemies," we have a chance to open our hearts and connect across some of our great divides.

In this book, the word *heart* reclaims its original meaning. "Heart" comes from the Latin *cor* and points not merely to our emotions but to the core of the self, that center place where all of our ways of knowing converge—intellectual, emotional, sensory, intuitive, imaginative, experiential, relational, and bodily, among others. The heart is where we integrate what we know in our minds with what we know in our bones, the place where our knowledge can become more fully human. *Cor* is also the Latin root from which we get the word *courage*. When all that we understand of self and world comes together in the center place called the heart, we are more likely to find the courage to act humanely on what we know.

The politics of our time is the "politics of the brokenhearted"—an expression that will not be found in the analytical vocabulary of political science or in the strategic rhetoric of political organizing. Instead, it is an expression from the language of human wholeness. There are some human experiences that only the heart can comprehend and only heart-talk can convey. Among them are certain aspects of politics, by which I mean the essential and eternal human effort to craft the common life on which we all depend. This is the politics that Lincoln practiced as he led from a heart broken open to the whole of what it means to be human—simultaneously meeting the harsh demands of political reality and nurturing the seeds of new life.

When *all* of our talk about politics is either technical or strategic, to say nothing of partisan and polarizing, we loosen or sever the human connections on which empathy, accountability, and democracy itself depend. If we cannot talk about politics in the language of the heart—if we cannot be publicly heartbroken, for example, that the wealthiest nation on earth is unable to summon the political will to end childhood hunger at home—how can we create a politics worthy of the human spirit, one that has a chance to serve the common good?

The link between language and empathy was explored by the comedian and social critic George Carlin in his classic minihistory of the various ways we have named the postwar condition of some soldiers:

> There's a condition in combat. Most people know about it. It's when
> a fighting person's nervous system has been stressed to its absolute
> peak and maximum. Can't take anymore input. The nervous system
> has either . . . snapped or is about to snap.

In World War I, Carlin goes on, "that condition was called shell shock. Simple, honest, direct language. Two syllables, shell shock. Almost sounds like the guns themselves." By World War II, the name had morphed into "battle fatigue. Four syllables now. Takes a little longer to say. Doesn't seem to hurt as much." Then came the Korean War, and the condition became operational exhaustion. "The humanity has been squeezed completely out of the phrase," Carlin comments. "Sounds like something that might happen to your car."

Then came Vietnam, and we all know what shell shock has been called ever since: post-traumatic stress disorder. Says Carlin,

> Still eight syllables, but we've added a hyphen! And the pain is com-
> pletely buried under jargon. . . . I'll bet you if we'd still been calling
> it shell shock, some of those Vietnam veterans might have gotten the
> attention they needed at the time.[7]

Carlin missed one precursor to shell shock, an important one in the context of this book. During the Civil War, traumatized combatants developed a condition that they called "soldier's heart."[8] The violence that results in soldier's heart shatters a person's sense of self and community, and war is not the only setting in which violence is done: violence is done whenever we violate another's integrity. Thus we do violence in politics when we demonize the opposition or ignore urgent human needs in favor of politically expedient decisions.

∞

This book, like the personal journey that helped shape it, does not blink at the darkness laced through American life today. Still, it is full of hope about our capacity to see the light. When I came out of my own darkness back into the light—to the people I love, the work I believe in, the world about which I care—the conflicts within and around me no longer tore me apart. With eyes wide open and a broken-open heart, I was better able to hold personal and political tensions in ways that generate insight, engagement, and new life.

Looking at politics through the eye of the heart can liberate us from seeing it as a chess game of moves and countermoves or a shell game for seizing power or a blame game of Whac-A-Mole. Rightly understood, politics is no game at all. It is the ancient and honorable human endeavor of creating a community in which the weak as well as the strong can flourish, love and power can collaborate, and justice and mercy can have their day. "We the People" must build a political life rooted in the commonwealth of compassion and creativity still found among us, becoming a civic community sufficiently united to know our own will and hold those who govern accountable to it.

In January 1838—when Abraham Lincoln was twenty-eight years old and the Civil War was twenty-three years off—a prescient Lincoln addressed the Young Men's Lyceum of Springfield, Illinois, on "the perpetuation of our political institutions." Exhorting his audience to understand the responsibility to protect American democracy against its enemies, he said:

> At what point shall we expect the approach of danger? . . . Shall
> we expect some transatlantic military giant, to step the Ocean, and
> crush us at a blow? Never! All the armies of Europe, Asia and Africa
> combined . . . could not by force, take a drink from the Ohio, or
> make a track on the Blue Ridge, in a Trial of a thousand years.

> At what point then is the approach of danger to be expected? I
> answer, if it ever reach us, it must spring up amongst us. It cannot
> come from abroad. If destruction be our lot, we must ourselves be its

author and finisher. As a nation of freemen, we must live through all time, or die by suicide.[9]

The Cold War made it clear that America was vulnerable to attacks from abroad despite the protection of two oceans, a fact underscored by the events of September 11, 2001. Still, Lincoln's case holds. If American democracy fails, the ultimate cause will not be a foreign invasion or the power of big money or the greed and dishonesty of some elected officials or a military coup or the internal communist/socialist/fascist takeover that keeps some Americans awake at night. It will happen because we—you and I—became so fearful of each other, of our differences and of the future, that we unraveled the civic community on which democracy depends, losing our power to resist all that threatens it and call it back to its highest form.

Our differences may be deep: what breaks my heart about America may make your heart sing, and vice versa. Protecting our right to disagree is one of democracy's gifts, and converting this inevitable tension into creative energy is part of democracy's genius. You and I may disagree profoundly on what constitutes a political failure or success, but we can still agree on this: democracy is always at risk. Government "of the people, by the people, and for the people" is a nonstop experiment in the strength and weakness of our political institutions, our local communities and associations, and the human heart. Its outcome can never be taken for granted.

The democratic experiment is endless, unless we blow up the lab, and the explosives to do the job are found within us. But so also is the heart's alchemy that can turn suffering into community, conflict into the energy of creativity, and tension into an opening toward the common good. We can help keep the experiment alive by repairing and maintaining democracy's neglected infrastructure, whose two levels are the primary concerns of this book: *the invisible dynamics of the human heart and the visible venues of our lives in which those dynamics are formed.*

It is well known and widely bemoaned that we have neglected our physical infrastructure—the roads, water supplies, and power grids on which our daily lives depend. Even more dangerous is our neglect of democracy's infrastructure, and yet it is barely noticed and rarely discussed. The heart's dynamics and the ways in which they are shaped lack the drama and the "visuals" to make the evening news, and restoring them is slow and daunting work. Now is the time to notice, and now is the time for the restoration to begin.

For those of us who want to see democracy survive and thrive—and we are legion—the heart is where *everything* begins: that grounded place in each of us where we can overcome fear, rediscover that we are members of one another, and embrace the conflicts that threaten democracy as openings to new life for us and for our nation.*

---

*In the course of writing this book, I have heard a good deal of debate on the question "Is the United States a democracy or a republic?" My answer is that it is both: we are a representative democracy set in the context of a constitutional republic. I give due attention in this book to the structures of our republic, one of whose most important functions is to protect the rights of individuals and minorities from being overwhelmed by the majority. But my primary focus is on the health of the democratic processes characterized by Lincoln in the Gettysburg Address as a "government of the people, by the people, for the people."

CHAPTER I

Democracy's Ecosystem

So, two cheers for Democracy: one because it admits variety and two because it permits criticism. Two cheers are quite enough: there is no occasion to give three.

—E. M. FORSTER, *Two Cheers for Democracy*[1]

The thing about democracy, beloveds, is that it is not neat, orderly, or quiet. It requires a certain relish for confusion.

—MOLLY IVINS, *You Got to Dance with Them What Brung You*[2]

For nearly an hour, we had been driving the back roads of southern Minnesota, past acre after acre of corn lined up in orderly, tedious, and mind-numbing rows. As we crested a hill, my friend broke the silence: "Check it out."

Afloat in the sea of uniformity called American agribusiness was an island of wind-blown grasses and wildflowers, a riot of colors and textures to delight the eye. We got out of the car and walked through this patch of prairie my friend had helped restore, dotted with the kinds of plants whose names make a found poem: wild four o'clock, bastard toadflax, Ohio horse mint, prairie Indian plantain. After some silence, my friend spoke again, saying something like this:

There are more than one hundred fifty species of plants on this prairie—to say nothing of the insects, birds, and mammals they attract—just as there were before we first broke the sod and started farming. It's beautiful, of course, but that's not the whole story. Biodiversity makes an ecosystem more creative, productive, adaptive to change, and resilient in the face of stress. The agribusiness land we've been driving through provides us with food and fuel. But we pay a very steep price for this kind of monoculture. It saps the earth's vitality and puts the quality and sustainability of our food supply at risk. The prairie as it once was—a state to which it can be restored—has a lot to teach us about how we need to live.

American democracy at its best is like that island of restored prairie. In a world where human diversity is often suppressed—where authoritarian regimes have kept people lined up like rows of cultivated corn, harvesting their labor and sometimes their lives to protect the interests of the state—the diversity that grows in a democracy delights the heart as well as the eye.

Our diversity consists only in part of demographic differences such as race, ethnicity, and social class. Equally important are the wildly different lenses through which we see, think, and believe. At the center of America's public life is a marketplace of ideas that only a free people could create, a vital, colorful, chaotic bazaar of religious, philosophical, political, and intellectual convictions. When democracy is working as it should, it is a complex and confusing mess where we can think and act as we choose, within the rule of law; can generate social and technological advances via the creative conflict of ideas; and can still manage to come together for the sake of the common good.

Just as a virgin prairie is less efficient than agribusiness land, democracy is less efficient than a dictatorship. We often move too slowly on matters of moral or practical urgency. And yet this loss of efficiency is more than offset by the way human diversity, freely expressed, can strengthen the body politic—offering resilience in the face of threat, adaptability to change, creativity and productivity in everything from commerce to science to culture.

I say *can*, not *will*, strengthen us because human beings have problems with diversity that have never vexed the wildflowers. A recent study by the political scientist Robert Putnam shows that demographic diversity can weaken a community's resourcefulness.[3] In the words of the journalist Michael Jonas, "The study, the largest ever on civic engagement in America, found that virtually all measures of civic health are lower in more diverse settings."[4]

Putnam's study tells us nothing new about human nature, which includes an ancient fear of "the other." In the face of diversity, we feel tension—and that, in turn, can lead to discomfort, distrust, conflict, violence, and even war. So we have developed a variety of strategies to evade our differences, strategies that only deepen our fear, such as associating exclusively with "our own kind" or using one of our well-tested methods to dismiss, marginalize, demonize, or eliminate the stranger. When our ancient fear of otherness is left unacknowledged, unattended, and untreated, diversity creates dysfunctional communities, as Putnam's study reminds us. The benefits of diversity can be ours only if we hold our differences with respect, patience, openness, and hope, which means we must attend to the invisible dynamics of the heart that are part of democracy's infrastructure.

For example, we regard "tension" as a condition to be relieved, not an energy to hold in our hearts. Tension creates stress, which leads to ill health, so we must reduce or eliminate these enemies of well-being. That is good advice if our stress comes from a toxic workplace, an abusive relationship, or some other assault on body or soul. But the stress that comes from being stretched by alien ideas, values, and experiences is of a different sort. This is why some psychologists distinguish between *distress* (which is negative and destructive), and *eustress* (which is positive and a prod to growth). It is important to know the difference. Positive stress may try our patience, and yet it can help our hearts become more spacious and generous. Refuse to hold stress of this sort, and our society as well as our souls will suffer from shrinkage and stagnation.

Once again, Abraham Lincoln offers a case in point. His life was laced with the stress that comes from being hounded by darkness; high anxiety and high blood pressure are among the well-known companions of depression. Lincoln had easy access to an array of popular therapies, such as opium, the water cure, or visits to a mesmerist. And yet he rejected all of these ways of numbing or evading the inner darkness that he needed to acknowledge, embrace, and integrate.[5]

For therapy, Lincoln turned instead to poetry and humor—poetry to reflect on the human condition and humor to keep it in perspective. In this way, as his biographer, Joshua Shenk, points out, Lincoln "did not dampen, but rather highlighted, the essential tension of his life."[6] He chose to engage rather than evade the sources of his stress. Evasion would have diverted him from "his desire to do something meaningful" with his life, draining him of energy for the pursuit.[7]

Diversity, Tension, and Democracy

When we choose to engage, not evade, the tension of our differences, we will become better equipped to participate in a government of, by, and for the people as we expand some of our key civic capacities:[8]

- To listen to each other openly and without fear, learning how much we have in common despite our differences
- To deepen our empathy for the alien "other" as we enter imaginatively into the experiences of people whose lives are radically unlike our own
- To hold what we believe and know with conviction *and* be willing to listen openly to other viewpoints, changing our minds if needed
- To seek out alternative facts and explanations whenever we find reason to doubt our own truth claims or the claims made by others, thus becoming better informed
- To probe, question, explore, and engage in dialogue, developing a fuller, more three-dimensional view of reality in the process
- To enter the conflicted arena of politics, able to hold the dynamics of that complex force field in ways that unite the civic community and empower us to hold government accountable to the will of the people

- To welcome opportunities to participate in collective problem solving and decision making, generating better solutions and making better decisions as we work with competing ideas[9]
- To feel more at home on the face of the earth amid differences of many sorts, better able to enjoy the fruits of diversity

Instincts and capacities like these allow us to make full use of the institutions of American democracy, institutions that were designed for creative tension-holding. From the separation of powers and system of checks and balances among the executive, legislative, and judicial branches to the tug-of-war between federal and state governments to our adversarial system of justice, American democracy was intended to generate, not suppress, the energy created by conflict, converting it into social progress as a hydroelectric plant converts the energy of dammed-up water into usable power.

But our democratic institutions are not automated. They must be inhabited by citizens and citizen leaders who know how to hold conflict inwardly in a manner that converts it into creativity, allowing it to pull them open to new ideas, new courses of action, and each other. That kind of tension-holding is the work of the well-tempered heart: if democracy is to thrive as that restored prairie is thriving, our hearts and our institutions must work in concert.

It will take me the rest of this book to explain what I mean by that claim and explore its implications. However, in less than five hundred words, I can tell you what you will *not* find in the pages to come:

• I will not prescribe a ten-step program that promises to teach the art of creative tension-holding. At the deepest levels of human life, we do not need techniques. We need insights into ourselves and our world that can help us understand how to learn and grow from our experiences of diversity, tension, and conflict. Just as Lincoln rejected the coping techniques of his time in favor of poetry and humor—which are doorways to understanding—this book attempts to offer insights that can help us hold tension well.

- I will say little about "them," the people in Washington, D.C., on whom we like to blame our ills. My focus is on "We the People," whose will is key to democracy. If we cannot come together with enough trust to discern the general will—and support leaders who are responsive to it while resisting the rest—we will forfeit the "Blessings of Liberty to ourselves and our Posterity."

- I will not complain at length about the clear and present danger to democracy posed by big money, although we need to pay close attention to those who do. As the journalist Bill Moyers has said, "The antidote, the only antidote, to the power of organized money in Washington is the power of organized people."[10]

- I will not plead for tolerance, a virtue so thin it is barely a virtue: "Be of good cheer! I am willing to tolerate you!" Nor will I spend much time pleading for better manners in public discourse: manners for the sake of manners are as thin as tolerance. The civility we need will not come from watching our tongues. It will come from valuing our differences.

- I will not ask us to dial down our differences. Democracy gives us the right to disagree and is designed to use the energy of creative conflict to drive positive social change. Partisanship is not a problem. Demonizing the other side is.

- I will not demand that we become better informed, though God knows we should. Research reveals that people who are shown solid evidence contradicting their most fundamental beliefs often become more forceful in advocating those beliefs.[11] We will *want* the information we need in order to come closer to the truth only when we stop fearing whatever might challenge our convictions and value it instead.

- I will not issue a call for a third-party movement. What we need is a popular movement that calls on the existing political parties to honor the will of the people. But as long as distrust and contempt keep "We the People" from having a generative conversation, our will cannot be known, let alone voiced.

I am not chasing the fantasy that some day we will "all get along." Given human nature and the nature of politics, there will always be people with whom dialogue is impossible—and on some days I am one of them. Suppose that those who can never be reached comprise 15 or 20 percent of both the left and the right, roughly the proportion of my own extended family with whom I cannot talk politics! That leaves 60 to 70 percent of us who *can* learn to talk across our differences; in a democracy, that is more than enough to save the day.

These "statistics," which come from the rather thin sample of my family, turn out to have historical warrant. Of the fifty-five delegates to the Constitutional Convention of 1787, only thirty-nine signed the final document.[12] The remaining 30 percent disagreed so deeply with one part or another of the Constitution that they took a pass on posterity.

Political divides such as these are nothing new in America. Still, the depth of political rancor today has many Americans worried about the future of our democracy. According to a 2010 poll that found widespread concern about the incivility of our civic life, 95 percent of Americans "believe civility in politics is important for a healthy democracy," and 87 percent "suggest it is possible for people to disagree about politics respectfully."[13]

The authors summarize their findings in these words:

> A core finding of our study is the potential long-term danger posed by the conduct of contemporary politics. We believe our study signals a warning: Americans do not like the way we are "doing politics," and they believe hostility and vitriol are signs of an ailing system. Several years ago, columnist and author E. J. Dionne Jr. noted that "a nation that hates politics will not long thrive as a democracy." We could not agree more.[14]

Truth, Suffering, and Hope

Heart, as I said in the Prelude, is a word that reaches far beyond our feelings. It points to a larger way of knowing—of receiving and reflecting on our experience—that goes deeper than the mind alone can take us. The heart is where we integrate the intellect with the rest of our faculties, such as emotion, imagination, and intuition. It is where we can learn how to "think the world together," not apart, and find the courage to act on what we know.

If you hold your knowledge of self and world wholeheartedly, your heart will at times get broken by loss, failure, defeat, betrayal, or death. What happens next in you and the world around you depends on *how* your heart breaks. If it breaks *apart* into a thousand pieces, the result may be anger, depression, and disengagement. If it breaks *open* into greater capacity to hold the complexities and contradictions of human experience, the result may be new life. The heart is what makes us human—and politics, which is the use of power to order our life together, is a profoundly human enterprise. Politics in the hands of those whose hearts have been broken open, not apart, helps us hold our differences creatively and use our power courageously for the sake of a more equitable, just, and compassionate world.

Despite my faith in what Lincoln, in his first inaugural, called the "better angels of our nature"—the beneficent powers that are released when our hearts break open—there are days when my hope for democracy's future wanes. Bill Moyers names some of the reasons why in his lament over the current state of our political system:

> Democracy in America is a series of narrow escapes, and we may be running out of luck. The reigning presumption about the American experience . . . is grounded in the idea of progress, the conviction that the present is "better" than the past and the future will bring even more improvements. For all of its shortcomings, we keep telling ourselves, "The system works."
>
> Now all bets are off. We have fallen under the spell of money, faction, and fear, and the great American experience in creating a different future together has been subjugated to individual cunning in the pursuit of wealth and power—and to the claims of empire with its ravenous demands and stuporous distractions. A sense of political impotence pervades the country—a mass resignation

defined by [the historian Lawrence] Goodwyn as "believing in the dogma of 'democracy' on a superficial public level but not believing it privately." . . . Hope no longer seems the operative dynamic of America, and without hope we lose the talent and drive to cooperate in the shaping of our destiny.[15]

Moyers's assessment is grim. And yet it is rich with the kind of truth-telling required if we are to regain hope and "cooperate in the shaping of our destiny"—democracy's destiny. And the truth is that Americans are suffering. We suffer from a widespread loss of jobs, homes, savings, and citizen confidence in our economic and political systems. We suffer from a fear of terrorism and the paranoia it produces. We suffer from a fragmentation of community that leaves us isolated from one another. We suffer, ironically, from our indifference to those among us who suffer. And we suffer as well from a hopeless sense that our personal and collective destinies are no longer in our hands.

What shall we do with our suffering? That is one of the most fateful questions human beings must wrestle with. Sometimes suffering rises into anger that leads to murder or war; at other times it descends into despair that leads to quick or slow self-destruction. Violence is what we get when we do not know what else to do with our suffering.

But when the human heart is open and allowed to work its alchemy, suffering can generate vitality instead of violence. This is a principle that Abraham Lincoln understood from the inside out. As Joshua Shenk comments:

From his early letters lamenting the "peculiar misfortune" of his temperament, to poetry he wrote on subjects such as suicide and madness, Lincoln's life sprang from a search for meaning that explained, and even ennobled, his affliction. As president, Lincoln urged his countrymen to accept their blessing and their burden, to see that their suffering had meaning, and to join him on a journey toward a more perfect Union.[16]

In my personal life, I have learned what millions have learned from crushing losses and defeats: such experiences, rightly held, can make us more compassionate and receptive, deepening our engagement with others and opening us to new life. The powers of the heart that transform personal anguish can also transform the way we do politics. The suffering that undermines democracy by driving us into foxholes and fragmenting the civic community has the potential to open us to each other, to hope, and to the hard work required to sustain the American experiment.

The John Woolman Story

If the "power of the broken heart" makes sense to you in the context of personal life but seems irrelevant to politics, consider this story of an ordinary citizen and an issue of great moral and political consequence that continues to haunt our democracy.

John Woolman (1720–1772) was a Quaker who lived in colonial New Jersey among other merchants and farmers in the Society of Friends whose affluence depended on enslaving human beings who, like them, had names and families, histories and hopes. Woolman, a tailor who did not own slaves, was torn by the blatant contradiction between the Quaker belief in human equality and the fact that many Quaker gentry were slaveholders. He refused to make that tension disappear by ignoring it, using theological sleight of hand, or riding its energy toward violence. Instead, he insisted that his community hold that tension with honesty and resolve it with integrity by freeing their slaves.

Quakers make decisions by consensus[17] instead of majority rule, and Woolman's local meeting (or congregation) was unable to reach unity on his proposal. Nonetheless, persuaded of Woolman's absolute integrity in the matter, they agreed to support him as he pursued his concern. For the next twenty years, Woolman made frequent trips up and down the East Coast, visiting Friends in their homes and their shops, at their farms, and in their meetings. He spoke with his fellow

Quakers about the heartbreaking contradiction between their faith and their practice. And he was always true to his beliefs. He wore undyed white clothing because dye was a product of slave labor; at meals, he would fast rather than eat food prepared or served by slaves, even if he stayed to talk; and if he learned that he had inadvertently benefited from a slave's work, he would pay that person his or her due without calling attention to the exchange.

Woolman and his family paid a great price for his consistent witness to truth's imperatives and his deeply felt heartbreak. Nonetheless, he held that tension, held it for twenty long years, until Quakers became the first religious community in America to free their slaves, some eighty years before the Civil War. In 1783, Quakers petitioned the Congress to correct the "complicated evils" and "unrighteous commerce" created by the enslavement of human beings.[18] And from 1827 onward, Quakers played a key role in developing the Underground Railroad, "an informal network of secret routes and safe houses used by nineteenth-century black slaves . . . to escape to free states and Canada with the aid of abolitionists who were sympathetic to their cause."[19]

These historic outcomes were possible because not just Woolman but the entire Quaker community held their internal contradiction consciously and constantly until they saw the light. The community, like Woolman himself, refused to resolve the matter falsely or prematurely. The Quakers did not take a quick vote to let the slave-owning majority have its way, nor did they banish the vexatious Woolman from their midst. They tested their convictions in dialogue and labored to achieve unity, trusting tension to do its work, until they finally arrived at a decision of historic proportions.

Sadly, members of the United States Congress were unwilling to hold the tension even long enough to consider the Quakers' petition of 1783. After hearing the petition read on October 8, they immediately tabled it and never took it up again. Perhaps there was too much tension in the fact that the petition invoked the Declaration of Independence, stating that the institution of slavery exists "in opposition to the solemn declaration often repeated in favor of universal liberty."[20]

John Woolman's story allows us to distinguish once more between two kinds of heartbreak. The first is the conventional image of a heart exploded into a thousand shards. Some of us try to pick up the pieces and put our lives back together; some fall into long-term despair; some take grim satisfaction in the injury the heart's explosion inflicts on our enemies. This kind of broken heart is an unresolved wound that keeps on wounding us and others. When the heart is brittle and shatters, it can scatter the seeds of violence and multiply our suffering among others.

And yet as Woolman's story reveals, there is an alternative image for a broken heart. When the heart is supple, it can be "broken open" into a greater capacity to hold our own and the world's pain: it happens every day. When we hold our suffering in a way that opens us to greater compassion, heartbreak becomes a source of healing, deepening our empathy for others who suffer and extending our ability to reach out to them. This kind of tension-holding can plant the seeds of justice and peace, as Woolman and other exemplars of nonviolence have shown time and again.[21]

The Woolman story also underscores a point that is critical to the central thesis of this book: holding tension creatively does *not* mean indecision or inaction. At every level of human life—from living our own lives well to governing a nation justly—decisions must be made. But they must not be made in the haste that comes from being impatient with tension or in the ignorance that results from fearing the clash of diverse opinions. If the Quaker way of getting eighty years ahead of the Civil War on America's greatest moral dilemma means anything at all, it means that the broken-open, tension-holding heart is not only a powerful source of compassion and healing. It is also a source of the wisdom required to make challenging decisions well.

The impulses that make democracy possible—and those that threaten it—originate in the heart, with its complex mix of heedless self-interest and yearning for community. From there, these impulses move out into our relations with each other in families, neighborhoods, workplaces, voluntary associations, and the various settings of public life. These are the places where John Woolman made a difference simply by walking and talking persistently *and* with principle. These are the places where we can make a difference, too, once we free ourselves from the illusion that we are at the mercy of forces beyond our control.

We normally associate "politics" with distant centers of power—legislatures, lobbyists, party caucuses, and board rooms—not with the everyday settings I just named. That is a mistake, for those places comprise the vital *prepolitical* layer of our common life, the social infrastructure on which democracy's well-being depends. At the highest levels of institutional politics, the common good is rarely served if citizens are not speaking and acting in these local venues, gathering the collective power necessary to support the best and resist the worst of our leaders as they decide on matters that affect all of us.

Democracy depends on ordinary Americans like John Woolman, energized rather than defeated by whatever breaks their hearts, taking step after small step in local settings to contribute to the commonweal.[22] As Howard Zinn wrote:

> The essential ingredients of [all] struggles for justice are human beings who, if only for a moment, if only while beset with fears, step out of line and do *something*, however small. And even the smallest, most unheroic of acts adds to the store of kindling that may be ignited by some surprising circumstance into tumultuous change.[23]

What Lies Ahead

In the chapters to come, I first want to deepen our understanding of what it means to practice politics from the heart. Within us is a yearning for something better than divisiveness, toxicity, passivity, powerlessness, and selling our democratic inheritance to the highest bidder. Within us is the courage to pursue that yearning, to hold life's tensions consciously, faithfully, and well, until they break us open.

The broken-open heart is a source of power as well as compassion—the power to bring down whatever diminishes us and raise up whatever serves us well. We can access and deploy that power by doing what every great social movement has done: *put time, skill, and energy into the education and mobilization of the powers of the heart*. As history consistently demonstrates, heart talk can yield actions just as practical as those driven by conventional forms of power.

In Chapter II, I recount some of my own journey as an American citizen. In the microcosm of my own life, I see both the darkness and the light that can be found in "We the People" writ large, reminding me that democracy is as much about *me*—and *us*—as it is the elusive *them* on whom we like to pin our problems. I introduce Alexis de Tocqueville, the French intellectual who wrote the classic *Democracy in America* after visiting the United States in 1831–1832. Early on, Tocqueville saw that American democracy would fail if generation after generation of citizens did not develop what he called the "habits of the heart" that democracy requires. By that phrase he meant deeply ingrained patterns of receiving, interpreting, and responding to experiences that involve our intellects, emotions, self-images, and concepts of meaning and purpose—habits that form the *inward and invisible infrastructure of democracy*. I name five of the habits we need if we are to hold the tuggings and tearings of life in a creative manner.

In Chapter III, I argue that the heart has always been a driver of politics, a source of inner power that gets harnessed for ends that range from good to evil. That power is amplified and released through the experience of heartbreak. But the kind of power generated depends on how the heart breaks—and the elasticity that allows it to break open instead of apart comes only through the exercise of democratic habits of the heart. In that chapter, I examine the inner emptiness of our time that manifests itself in consumerism and scapegoating, two underlying "heart conditions" we must combat if we are to develop the habits of the heart that a democracy demands.

Having made a case for role of the heart in politics, I devote the next four chapters to examining the *outward and visible infrastructure of democracy,* those spaces and settings of everyday life in which habits of the heart are formed, for better or for worse. I propose practical, on-the-ground possibilities for making better use of these venues to learn how to hold our differences in a manner that can restore "We the People."

In Chapter IV, I look at humanity's long history of resisting the "fight or flight" response by inventing institutions devoted to creative tension-holding. The governing structures created by America's founders are the crowning political achievement of this history, which will function as intended if and only if they are inhabited by people who have learned to hold tension in their hearts. Here I explore the hopeful fact that many of us find our hearts opened by the tensions of personal life and can learn to take that capacity into the public realm.

In Chapter V, I examine the public life, our everyday movement to and fro "in the company of strangers." I explore its role in a democracy, the sources of its decline, and how we can rebuild this crucial prepolitical layer of life where the heart gets formed or deformed, almost without our knowledge. Public life is so commonplace that we take it for granted, as we do our air and water. And yet a healthy democracy is as dependent on public life as a healthy ecosystem is dependent on clean air and water: in the absence of an engaged public, democracy begins to die, and some form of oligarchy emerges to take its place.

In Chapter VI, I explore some of the traditional settings in which habits of the heart can be cultivated consciously and intentionally, such as public schools, colleges and universities, and religious communities. I propose practical ways in which these institutions, so crucial to a democracy, can reclaim their historic function of forming citizens in local settings that range from classrooms to congregations.

In Chapter VII, I examine the unsafe political space created by the mass media, a space so vast, fragmented, and frenzied that dwelling in it too long makes us feel powerless. Then I look at nontraditional spaces where citizens can find the safety to reclaim their individual and collective power. These include spaces of silence and solitude where we can remember who we are, small face-to-face circles of the sort familiar to community organizers, and certain forms of online community. In these human-scale settings, we can resist the deformations of the mass media and find the sense of voice and agency that citizenship requires.

Finally, in Chapter VIII, I take one last look at the role of the heart in human history. The history of the heart cannot be written by observing world events, but we can find important clues to it by examining the national myths that express our aspirations. I spell out the process by which social movements, including the movement called democracy, have tried to narrow the gap between aspiration and reality. Then I revisit the concept of creative tension-holding by exploring our need to stand and act in the "tragic gap," the gap that will forever separate what *is* from what *could* and *should* be. The courage to inhabit this gap with energy, commitment, vision, and hope has been a driver of all great human experiments to fulfill the heart's aspirations, not least the experiment called America.

If we want to reclaim democracy's "base"—not the base that political parties must rally to win elections but "We the People" who form the foundation of American democracy itself—we need good information and all the rationality we can muster.[24] And yet that will not be enough. We must also develop intentional and intelligent approaches for educating and engaging the human heart, the source of what Lincoln called "the better angels of our nature" on which democracy depends.

Amid our current struggles, it is worth remembering the context in which Lincoln spoke those words that ended his first inaugural address on March 4, 1861.[25] It was a moment in American history when it seemed highly unlikely that the Union could endure, and the only enemy in sight was us. Five weeks later, the first shots of the Civil War were fired at Fort Sumter. Four murderous years after that, with 620,000 military casualties and a civilian death toll estimated at 50,000, Lee surrendered to Grant at Appomattox.

At the moment Lincoln spoke, with the nation on the brink of such massive violence, his hopeful words about "angels" must have seemed like a futile gesture, and a pitiful one at that, a thimbleful of oil tossed onto a raging sea in the vain hope of calming it. Still, it was exactly the kind of moment—a moment of hopelessness that presaged many more

of the same—when only hope deeply rooted in a broken-open heart
can see us through:

> We are not enemies, but friends. We must not be enemies. Though
> passion may have strained it must not break our bonds of affection.
> The mystic chords of memory, stretching from every battlefield and
> patriot grave to every living heart and hearthstone all over this broad
> land, will yet swell the chorus of the Union, when again touched, as
> surely they will be, by the better angels of our nature.

CHAPTER II

Confessions of an Accidental Citizen

It's coming to America first,
the cradle of the best and of the worst.
It's here they got the range
and the machinery for change
and it's here they got the spiritual thirst.
It's here the family's broken
and it's here the lonely say
that the heart has got to open
in a fundamental way:
Democracy is coming to the U.S.A.

—LEONARD COHEN, "Democracy"[1]

As a white, male American who has always been well-off—the kind of person for whom this nation has always worked best—the gift of full citizenship, unquestioned and unchallenged, came to me as an accident of birth. Today I realize the magnitude of that gift. But for years I was an unconscious and ungrateful recipient because attaining citizenship required no effort from me.

I grew up in the 1950s, politically quiescent years for people of "my kind." My political education began in 1961, the year I graduated from college, when I heard John F. Kennedy speak those famous words, "Ask not what your country can do for you; ask what you can do for your country." During the 1960s, as a married graduate student with a growing family, I began to become more aware of the gift I had been given, began to inquire more actively into what my citizenship might mean. In the challenging years that followed—filled as they were with assassinations, ill-conceived wars, and the cruelties of injustice at home and abroad—I had my first experiences of political heartbreak. And yet if you had asked me during those years which of my several roles was most important to me, I would have named parent, spouse, teacher, writer, and whatever income-earning job I had at the time. Citizen would not have been on my list.

I do not mean that one cannot be a citizen in those other roles. On the contrary, there is vital citizen work to be done in all of them, as I hope to show in this book. When we reduce the citizen role to a narrow band of partisan political activities that many people do not find engaging or even possible—such as joining and contributing to a political party, going door-to-door for a candidate, or participating in rallies—our chances of achieving full citizenship are diminished. Most of us will be citizens primarily in the everyday venues of family, work, and local community.

Still, in my late twenties and on into midlife, my awareness of what it means to be a citizen was diminished, even distorted, by my failure to understand that *how* I played my everyday prepolitical roles could help meet democracy's needs. I wanted to contribute to the common good, but what was good for me and mine came first. I spent five years working as a community organizer, but that was partly because I wanted an unconventional career. I wrote a book on the renewal of America's public life, but I was strongly motivated by a need to put my unconventional career on someone's radar before I fell off the edge of the known world.[2]

Citizenship and the Common Good

There was nothing inimical to democracy in the way I made my living or in my conception of what was good for me and mine. I did not run drugs or imagine that my family and I were entitled to a life of luxury; indeed, for many years we lived fairly low on the hog. Still, take a job that does not diminish the common good, mix in the pursuit of private interests that are harmless to others, and the result is "citizenship lite." In twenty-first-century America, lite will not do—not if we want democracy to survive, let alone thrive.

Today, in my early seventies, I look at citizenship differently than I did when I was young. Time has stripped me of some of my more specialized roles, and soon enough I will be playing no role at all. Now I see a deeper truth about the meaning of citizenship: it cannot be reduced to the roles we play. Today, my definition of citizenship is deep-seated and wide-reaching: *Citizenship is a way of being in the world rooted in the knowledge that I am a member of a vast community of human and nonhuman beings that I depend on for essentials I could never provide for myself.*

I see now that I have no choice—at least, no honorable choice—except to affirm, celebrate, and express my gratitude for that community in every aspect of my life, trying to be responsive to its needs whether or not my immediate self-interests are met. Whatever is in the common good is, in the long run, good for me and mine.

But if I believe in the importance of that community, I cannot afford to let my vision of citizenship drift off into a romantic fantasy about the body politic as a place where everyone agrees that there *is* a common good, let alone on *what* it is. Political life in a democracy is too gritty, imperfect, and conflicted for that. Glossing over our differences diminishes democracy's potential: those differences are grist for democracy's mill, if we know how to hold them in life-giving ways.

I will not pretend that I find it easy to embrace this fact. Get me going on politicians who distort my faith tradition to win votes or on racial bigots and homophobes who want to translate their personal shadows into public policy, and this nice Quaker boy from the Midwest does a passable imitation of the Incredible Hulk. Still, no matter how jaw-dropping or morally offensive I find some people's convictions, I must learn how to speak up in the civic community without denying my opponents their humanity and further poisoning the political ecosystem on which democracy depends.

Even if we could achieve respectful discourse, I doubt that we could reach widespread agreement on the details of the common good: Americans are deeply divided on issues ranging from supporting public education to financing health care to the role of government itself. We may not be able to agree on the details, but if we believe in our form of government, we *must* agree on an alternative definition that makes preserving democracy itself the focus of our concern. We must be able to say, in unison: *It is in the common good to hold our political differences and the conflicts they create in a way that does not unravel the civic community on which democracy depends.*

My understandings of citizenship and the common good are rooted in three beliefs I have held, with varying degrees of conviction, over the past forty years—beliefs that were more theoretical and less embodied in my youth than they are for me today:

- I believe in democracy—in its indisputable achievements and its unfulfilled promise.
- I believe in American political institutions—in the genius inherent in their design and in the undeniable good they have done when put to their best use.
- I believe in the power of the human heart—in its capacity for truth and justice, love and forgiveness.

These beliefs may seem unexceptional, even pious. That is not how I have experienced my lengthy struggle to hold them and live by them. American democracy and the human heart are so complex and contradictory that I have argued about my beliefs for years, sometimes with other people and more often with myself. I value the argument as much as I value the beliefs. "There are three kinds of patriots," said William Sloane Coffin, "two bad, one good. The bad are the uncritical lovers and the loveless critics. Good patriots carry on a lover's quarrel with their country."[3]

Faith and Doubt in Politics

History reveals that beliefs such as those I just named can become dangerous delusions if they are held uncritically. A brief glimpse at their shadow sides will prove the point:

- I believe in democracy. But what passes for democracy sometimes turns out to be a cover for something less noble, at home and abroad. At home we have deprived people of their freedom for reasons ranging from racism to economic exploitation to a simple failure to care. Abroad we have proved ourselves shameless about using our military might to "impose freedom" on people who do not want us occupying their country, claiming to advance democracy's cause when in fact we are protecting our economic interests at the expense of their lives.

- I believe in American political institutions. But those institutions too often set policy in response to the will of corporate power instead of the will of the people, who have a hard time making their will known without the access money can buy. And when the will of the people manages to make itself known, on the streets or at the ballot box, political leaders who think otherwise have a thousand ways to drag their feet, renege on their promises, or work backstage to protect their own and their sponsors' interests.

- I believe in the power of the human heart. But that power often runs amok, as with terrorism of various sorts, including the kind that cloaks itself with theological rationales. Or look at the media hatemongers who become celebrity millionaires by shading and twisting the truth, sometimes lying outright, then shouting down or defaming anyone who challenges them, weakening the trust on which democracy depends. Of course, they would not become rich and famous if our hearts did not harbor fear, resentment, and anger, making us into a market of addicts for what the hatemongers peddle.

So I need to parse my beliefs with more precision. I believe in *democracy* as long as we understand that it is not something we *have* but something we must *do*. However, I do not believe that American-style democracy is the cure-all for the problems of every nation on earth, especially when the people involved do not actively want it. Truth be told, I sometimes wonder how much we Americans want it. At the moment—as we allow the tension of our differences to fragment the civic community, creating a void that undemocratic powers are eager to fill—we are squandering our political inheritance as if it did not matter.

I believe in the *institutions of American democracy* when they function as the founders intended. Those men were tragically misguided when they excluded women, Native Americans, and enslaved human beings from the "We" in "We the People" and from the "all" in "all men are created equal." Obviously, they did not consciously lay the foundations for the diversity we have today. They would have been incredulous if someone had told them that all Americans over the age of eighteen (except for convicted felons) would eventually have the right to vote, and that by 2050 people of color would constitute half of all Americans.[4]

Nonetheless, the founders created political institutions that— energized by the periodic clamoring of vigilant Americans—have created a more inclusive society than most of them could have imagined or even deemed desirable. Today, nearly two and a half centuries after they left us their flawed legacy, what matters most is not the founders' racism, sexism, and elitism. What matters is the fact that without the institutions they gave us, it is unlikely that we would have the diversity with which we are now blessed, nor would we be able to harness the continuing tension between America's vision and reality for the sake of the common good.

Harness it we must, especially in relation to the struggle for racial justice, where we have made less progress than we like to think and have arguably reversed course. As the legal scholar Michelle Alexander has shown, the politically motivated "war on drugs"—with its racially biased enforcement and excessively harsh penalties for nonviolent, victimless crimes—has resulted in the fact that

> today there are more African Americans under correctional control, whether in prison or jail, on probation or on parole, than there were enslaved in 1850. And more African American men are disenfranchised now because of felon disenfranchisement laws than in 1870.[5]

I believe in the *power of the human heart* to do evil as well as good. The heart leads some to become terrorists and others to serve the hungry and the homeless. The heart leads some to blow up federal buildings in order to "bring down the government" and others to see that *we are* the government and must work together to fulfill democracy's promise. The heart is a complex force field, no less complex than democracy itself, a maelstrom of conflicted powers that we ignore, sentimentalize, or dismiss at our peril.

Abraham Lincoln, with his fundamental faith in "the better angels of our nature," knew through personal experience that those angels had shadowy companions. As his biographer, Joshua Shenk, comments, Lincoln's image of our better angels

> contains within it a sense of perpetual complexity, of lasting tension. Individuals and nations are multifaceted, capable of better and prone to worse, ever locked in struggle. "Better angels of our nature," as with many of Lincoln's phrases, reaches deep into the human psyche, because it reflects an experience that every human being knows intuitively, one of division and conflict, brokenness and harmony, suffering and reward, a journey and its challenges.[6]

The human heart, this vital core of the human self, holds the power to destroy democracy or to make it whole. That is why our nineteenth-century visitor, Alexis de Tocqueville, insisted in his classic *Democracy in America* that democracy's future would depend heavily on generations of American citizens cultivating the habits of the heart that support political wholeness.

As Tocqueville scholar Leo Damrosch points out, the basic theme of Tocqueville's two-volume work is that "habits and beliefs are more important than laws are in sustaining liberty."[7] Walt Whitman, the poet laureate of American democracy, agreed. His poem "States!"—referring to the United States—begins with these lines:

> STATES!
> Were you looking to be held together by the lawyers?
> By an agreement on a paper? Or by arms?
>
> Away!
> I arrive, bringing these, beyond all the forces of courts and arms,
> These! to hold you together as firmly as the earth itself is held
> together.[8]

What Whitman means by "These!"—these powers that are "beyond all the forces of courts and arms"—is, very simply, the human relationships that are forged in the heart. If democracy is to work as it should and as it must, claimed Whitman, it will depend on "countless linked hands" across the land.

Today, amid the divisiveness that weakens our sense of community and threatens our democracy, a condition that neither law nor force can heal, it is clear that Tocqueville and Whitman were prophetic. If "We the People" are to hold democracy's tensions in ways that reweave the civic community, we must develop habits that allow our hearts to break open and embrace diversity rather than break down and further divide us.

Hearts Broken Open to Hope

In the spring of 1974, I had an experience that brought this imperative home to me personally and with power. I took a train from my home in Maryland to Americus, Georgia, where I spent a week at Koinonia Partners, birthplace of Habitat for Humanity. Located in Georgia's famous red clay country, the Koinonia community is dedicated to helping residents of that region escape the ravages of rural poverty by providing agricultural jobs and affordable housing.

I remember that red clay well because the white socks I wore as I walked those fields never lost their pink tint. Even more indelible is the memory of a few hours I spent one Sunday morning with a handful of people at a small independent black church a few miles down the road. The parishioners, many of whom lived in shacks and eked out a living working other people's land, came from generations of suffering caused by America's betrayal of its own profession that "all men are created equal."

I arrived at church early to attend the adult Sunday school class that preceded the worship service. Though I do not remember the topic being discussed, I will never forget the way the class was conducted. Only three members were present that morning. Still, these three ran the class as they always did, by Robert's Rules of Order, a set of procedures that helps groups make decisions in an orderly manner while avoiding stalemates and free-for-alls.[9] One member of the class served as presiding clerk, another as recording clerk, and the other as sergeant-at-arms—in case either of the others got out of hand, or so I supposed.

I was young then, as white as I am today, walled-off as much as well-off, educated without knowing much—and I was baffled. When I met with the pastor after the worship service, I blurted out, "I don't get it. Why did they have to run the Sunday school class so formally? Why couldn't they just sit and talk to each other?"

"Well," he said, "if you don't get *that,* there's probably a lot you don't get," a comment that got my attention. I did not take notes, so I cannot reproduce his comments verbatim, and yet the imprint of what I learned that morning remains strong to this day:

> The people who belong to this church are American citizens who have a long history of being deprived of their rights and shut out of the political process. Thanks to civil rights legislation, those doors are now open to them.

Roadblocks remain, of course, and will for a long time. But now our parishioners can speak up at caucuses, testify at hearings, make their needs and aspirations known to legislators, and do all the things that other citizens do to get their voices heard in the halls of power. As they move into the larger world, we want them to know what it's like to participate in a formal discussion or debate so they will not feel intimidated by what's out there. Robert's Rules of Order gives them a taste of that.

The people in that Sunday school class already know how to be good citizens by attending to each other's needs in their own community. They take the Bible seriously and care for the widow, the orphan, the hungry, and the homeless. Now they are practicing yet another form of citizenship—learning how to listen well, speak clearly, and follow procedures in the larger, more diverse, and conflicted world of American politics. Please remember what you learned today, and take it to heart.[10]

The people I met that morning were not "accidental citizens." The unchallenged rights of American citizenship had not come easily to them as they had to me. They valued their citizenship as people value something that has been hard-won. Even during their Sabbath rest from lives of manual labor, the members of that church worked away at the habits of the heart on which good citizenship depends.

The Story Behind the Story

These parishioners already possessed several well-developed habits that are key to sustaining democracy. They were, for example, community builders among the people they knew best: as their pastor testified, they stayed aware of and responsive to their neighbors' needs.

But democracy demands that we become engaged with "the other" as well as with "our own kind," with the stranger whose viewpoint, needs, and interests are likely to be different from our own. So the people I met in Americus spent time learning Robert's Rules of Order—a way of doing business that acclimates people to the culture of formality found in legislative bodies, settings from which these parishioners were once excluded. As they learned the logic of these formal rules, they were also cultivating informal habits of the heart—the habits required in order to speak up *and* listen to people of diverse opinions and to negotiate significant differences about problems, priorities, and solutions.

Long before these parishioners began learning Robert's Rules of Order, they had cultivated another habit of the heart that is key to creating community with people who are not of our tribe: a spirit of hospitality to the stranger. For evidence, look no farther than the warm welcome they gave me, a stranger who bore all the external marks of the overlords who had oppressed them since the founding of this country. No habit of the heart is more crucial to making "We the People" a reality than extending hospitality to those who appear alien to us.

Equally crucial is a habit called hope. Despite generations of oppression, these people held on to hope of several sorts: hope for the democracy that had promised them much and delivered little, hope for their own potential as citizens who could make a difference, and hope for people like me that we might even yet gain access to "the better angels of our nature." Hope had enabled them to hold the tension between the American value of human equality and the reality of the unjust and inhumane treatment they had suffered in this "land of the free" from the day the first of their ancestors was captured, chained, and brought to these shores. Time and again, generation after generation, their hearts had been broken by this contradiction. But instead of allowing that history to explode their hearts in fury or despair, they had let it break their hearts open to each other, to "the other," and to hope.

The wellspring of their hope was in a religious tradition that I happen to share. So when we met at church that day, we met in a context of shared belief that went deeper than our differences. It was a context so strong that neither my ignorance nor my arrogance could breach it, allowing the pastor to teach me rather than toss me out. Today, the public image of the Christian tradition is often one of creating divides, not bridging them, and the same is true of Judaism and Islam.

All three traditions are misunderstood because some of their alleged adherents engage in hateful and violent behavior that distorts and defiles the values they claim to represent. At their core, Christianity, Islam, Judaism, and all of the major world religions are committed to compassion and hospitality. As the religious historian Karen Armstrong has written, "All the world faiths insist that true spirituality must be expressed consistently in practical compassion, the ability to *feel with* the other."[11] In this fact lies the hope that we might reclaim their power to help reweave our tattered civic fabric.

For nearly four decades, the brief experience I had at a tiny independent black church in the red clay countryside of Georgia has been teaching me things I need to know. The hospitality extended to me by the parishioners and the lesson I was given by their pastor reveal the heart at its best, transforming the profound tensions of life in a flawed democracy into an energy of possibility that weaves community, animates creativity, and keeps the American promise alive.

In a few hours at that church, I learned at least as much about the heart of the citizen as I have learned from years spent among people who look and think like me. Some of what we must learn if democracy is to flourish comes only from "crossing over" into lives unlike our own, not fleeing from them in fear but entering into them in trust that an experience of "otherness" can help our closed hearts break open.

Tocqueville in America

Alexis de Tocqueville—whose travels took him to Knoxville, Georgia, fifty-five miles from Americus—would be glad to know that the habits of the heart he cared about were still alive and well in 1974 and being nurtured in a church. A century and a half earlier, he had seen voluntary associations such as churches as crucial elements of democracy's infrastructure.

Tocqueville would also be happily astonished to learn that the descendants of slaves had become American citizens. He saw slavery as a moral abomination that threatened our democracy and was not sure we could surmount its stain, a question that remains unresolved today. Though I grieve the fact that we continue to fall short of our own professed values—and have arguably backtracked on racial justice in recent years, notwithstanding the fact that we now have an African American president—I celebrate the fact that we have structures of political life that compel us to keep working on this contradiction.[12]

When Tocqueville toured America in the 1830s and saw the importance of democratic habits of the heart, he used the word *heart* in the same sense I use it here, as the integrative core of all the human faculties. As a synonym for the habits that concerned him, he uses the sociological term *mores* (*mœurs*), which refers, he says, not only to the emotions

> but also to the various notions that men possess, to the diverse opinions that are current among them, and to the whole range of ideas that shape habits of the mind. Thus I use this word to refer to the whole moral and intellectual state of a people.[13]

For Tocqueville, as Leo Damrosch points out, "ideas are at least as important as feelings, for without them 'there is no action in common, and without action in common there are only people, not a social body. For there to be a society, and still more for that society to prosper, the minds of its citizens must be brought together and held together by certain leading ideas.'"[14]

Tocqueville was especially concerned about the American habit of the heart he called "individualism," which he defines as "a calm and considered feeling which disposes each citizen to isolate himself from the mass of his fellows and withdraw into the circle of family and friends; with this little society formed to his taste, he gladly leaves the greater society to look after itself."[15] As social equality spreads and individualism grows, he wrote,

> there are more and more people who, though neither rich nor powerful enough to have much hold over others, have gained or kept enough wealth and enough understanding to look after their own

needs. Such folk owe no man anything and hardly expect anything from anybody. They form the habit of thinking of themselves in isolation and imagine their whole destiny is in their hands.[16]

The greater our tendency toward individualism, the weaker our communal fabric; the weaker our communal fabric, the more vulnerable we are to despotic power. Tocqueville's hope that the communal instinct might provide a counterbalance to American individualism and help us avoid the danger of despotism was based on the vigor he observed in religious, civic, and other forms of organizational life. "Americans of all ages, all conditions, and all dispositions," he wrote,

> constantly form associations. They have not only commercial and manufacturing companies, in which all take part, but associations of a thousand other kinds, religious, moral, serious, futile, general or restricted, enormous or diminutive. The Americans make associations to give entertainments, to found seminaries, to build inns, to construct churches, to diffuse books, to send missionaries to the antipodes; in this manner they found hospitals, prisons, and schools. If it is proposed to inculcate some truth or to foster some feeling by the encouragement of a great example, they form a society.[17]

In these associations, Tocqueville observed, "feelings and opinions are recruited, the heart is enlarged, and the human mind is developed, only by the reciprocal influence of men upon each other."[18]

He contrasts this feature of America to life in his own country. Prior to the French Revolution, voluntary associations were virtually unknown in France; the upper class held all the cards when it came to shaping public opinion, mounting social action, and forming policy. The *bourgeoisie* kept tight control of the game and held their cards close to the vest. But in America, Tocqueville saw citizens dealing themselves in and playing their own hands, providing a counterweight to central power by associating actively with one another and in the process cultivating the habits of the heart on which democracy depends.[19]

Twenty-first-century America is vastly different from the nation Tocqueville visited in the 1830s, different in size, urbanization, communications, diversity, national wealth, class structure, noise level, complexity, and global entanglements. And yet the dynamics of the human heart do not change dramatically over the course of time, and prominent among them is the tug-of-war between our need to be independent and our need to be interdependent. Today, nearly two centuries after Tocqueville observed our young democracy, Americans continue to vacillate between these poles.

Individualism remains a strong theme among us, supporting original thought and action, even against the crowd. Communalism continues to be a major influence in American life—though the forms it takes have changed since Tocqueville's time—offering us more prepolitical opportunities than the people of any nation have and thus more potential for political power.[20]

These habits have a downside as well, as does everything human: individualism can slip into selfishness, and communalism can collapse into having no mind of one's own. Learning how to hold individualism and communalism in creative tension with each other—allowing each to check the other's darker potentials—is a key democratic habit of the heart.

Five Habits of the Heart

If I were asked for two words to summarize the habits of the heart American citizens need in response to twenty-first-century conditions, *chutzpah* and *humility* are the words I would choose. By *chutzpah* I mean knowing that I have a voice that needs to be heard and the right to speak it.[21] By *humility* I mean accepting the fact that my truth is always partial and may not be true at all—so I need to listen with openness and respect, especially to "the other," as much as I need to speak my own voice with clarity and conviction. Humility plus chutzpah equals the kind of citizens a democracy needs. There is no reason, at least no *good* reason, why our number cannot be legion.

Of course, it takes more than two words to name the qualities we need today. Here are five interlocking habits of the heart—the first three relate to humility, the last two to chutzpah. Such habits (to repeat my earlier definition) are deeply ingrained patterns of receiving, interpreting, and responding to experience that involve our intellects, emotions, self-images, and concepts of meaning and purpose. These five habits, taken together, are crucial to sustaining a democracy.

• *We must understand that we are all in this together.* Ecologists, economists, ethicists, philosophers of science, and religious and secular leaders have all given voice to this theme. Despite our illusions of individualism and national superiority, we humans are a profoundly interconnected species—entwined with one another and with all forms of life, as the global economic and ecological crises reveal in vivid and frightening detail. We must embrace the simple fact that we are dependent on and accountable to one another, and that includes the stranger, the "alien other." At the same time, we must save this notion of interdependence from the idealistic excesses that make it an impossible dream. Exhorting people to hold a continual awareness of global or national interconnectedness is a counsel of perfection, achievable (if at all) only by the rare saint, that can only result in self-delusion or defeat. Which leads to a second key habit of the heart. . . .

• *We must develop an appreciation of the value of "otherness."* It is true that we are all in this together. It is equally true that we spend most of our lives in "tribes" or lifestyle enclaves—and that thinking of the world in terms of "us" and "them" is one of the many limitations of the human mind. The good news is that "us *and* them" does not need to mean "us *versus* them." Instead, it can remind us of the ancient tradition of hospitality to the stranger and give us a chance to translate it into twenty-first-century terms. Hospitality rightly understood is premised on the notion that the stranger has much to teach us. It actively invites "otherness" into our lives to make them more expansive, including forms of otherness that seem utterly alien to our way of life. Of course, we will not practice deep hospitality if we do not embrace the creative possibilities inherent in our differences. Which leads to a third key habit of the heart. . . .

• *We must cultivate the ability to hold tension in life-giving ways.* Our lives are filled with contradictions—from the gap between our aspirations and our behavior to observations and insights we cannot abide because they run counter to our convictions. If we fail to hold them creatively, these contradictions will shut us down and take us out of the action. But when we allow their tensions to expand our hearts, they can open us to new understandings of ourselves and our world, enhancing our lives and allowing us to enhance the lives of others. We are imperfect and broken beings who inhabit an imperfect and broken world. The genius of the human heart lies in its capacity to use these tensions to generate insight, energy, and new life. Making the most of those gifts requires a fourth key habit of the heart. . . .

• *We must generate a sense of personal voice and agency.* Insight and energy give rise to new life as we speak and act, expressing our version of truth while checking and correcting it against the truths of others. But many of us lack confidence in our own voices and in our power to make a difference. We grow up in educational and religious institutions that treat us as members of an audience instead of actors in a drama, and as a result we become adults who treat politics as a spectator sport. And yet it remains possible for us, young and old alike, to find our voices, learn how to use them, and know the satisfaction that comes from contributing to positive change—if we have the support of a community. Which leads to a fifth and final habit of the heart. . . .

• *We must strengthen our capacity to create community.* Without a community, it is nearly impossible to achieve voice: it takes a village to raise a Rosa Parks. Without a community, it is nearly impossible to exercise the "power of one" in a manner that multiplies: it took a village to translate Parks's act of personal integrity into social change. In a mass society like ours, community rarely comes ready-made. But creating community in the places where we live and work does not mean abandoning other parts of our lives to become full-time organizers. The steady companionship of two or three kindred spirits can kindle the courage we need to speak and act as citizens.

Holding Hands and Climbing

Cultivating these five habits may sound like an absurdly large task. In fact, it is a human-scale agenda within the reach of ordinary Americans in the ordinary venues of our lives: every one of these habits was under cultivation at that tiny independent black church in Americus, Georgia. Democracy needs a million "little platoons" of people like that one, scattered across the country, places where we can develop the personal and collective qualities democracy requires.[22] In the course of the next four chapters, I suggest in practical detail how we can do exactly that in the everyday settings of our lives.

The parishioners I met in Americus, Georgia, in the spring of 1974 invite—indeed, challenge—us to become intentional, not accidental, citizens. They embody virtues that give America some of its finest qualities: generosity of spirit, hope for the future, and the wit and will to work for the common good. They remind us of America's failures and give us reason to hope for its future, if we can learn the lessons of the broken-open heart. Grounded in that place of truth and hope, we can reach across the lines that divide us as those parishioners did, rebuilding the civic community required if "government of the people, by the people, for the people" is not to "perish from the earth."

In his poem "A Great Need,"[23] the thirteenth-century Persian poet Hafiz uses imagery reminiscent of Walt Whitman's mid-eighteenth-century call for "countless linked hands" to secure national unity.[24] Both of these poets speak to us about the current crisis of American democracy and what it demands of us. Both of them remind us that this is not the first time that threats to the common good have called us to hang on and hang together—and that we have the power to do just that in our hands and in our hearts:

Out
Of a great need
We are all holding hands
And climbing.
Not loving is a letting go.
Listen,
The terrain around here
Is
Far too
Dangerous
For
That.

CHAPTER III

The Heart of Politics

The human heart is the first home of democracy. It is where we embrace our questions. Can we be equitable? Can we be generous? Can we listen with our whole beings, not just our minds, and offer our attention rather than our opinions? And do we have enough resolve in our hearts to act courageously, relentlessly, without giving up—ever—trusting our fellow citizens to join with us in our determined pursuit of a living democracy?

—TERRY TEMPEST WILLIAMS, "Engagement"[1]

I came across these words about a "living democracy" as I was emerging from the dark passage of personal and political heartbreak I wrote about in the Prelude. Republicans happened to be in power at the time, but Democrats have broken my heart too, proving that it is a bad idea politically as well as personally to go looking for love in all the wrong places.

Following the terrorist attacks of September 11, 2001, America went to war. Our leaders either misled us about the rationale or were themselves duped, and they surreptitiously suspended some of our constitutional rights. Several leaders, including the president, urged us to be patriotic by going shopping, promoting consumerism to restore our economy rather than citizenship to restore our democracy. Many Americans supported the war. Many others expressed strong public disagreement. And yet no matter what case the protesters made, very few people in power appeared to be listening with anything like respect.

Our leaders seemed to disparage, not value, the diverse voices of "We the People." Some of them actively denigrated dissent. As citizens, we did not know how to frame and mount a civil debate on the momentous issue of war in a manner that would allow us to help set our country's direction. Incivility and incompetence reigned on the left, in the center, and on the right, or so it seemed to me. I was, to put it mildly, in a slough of despond. I was also in a self-imposed exile from my country's political life, convinced that I was powerless to resist the distortions of the democracy I love.

Terry Tempest Williams's words about democracy uplifted me with the reminder that none of us is powerless: if the heart is democracy's first home, then each of us has a share of the power required to call democracy back to its roots. But even as her words restored me, they also rebuked me: I had not been holding the questions Williams names— questions about my capacity for citizenship—with openness, honesty, trust, and persistence. I had allowed my heart to harden and had lost faith in my fellow citizens. The uplift *and* the upbraiding I found in Williams's words sparked a resolve to reclaim my active citizenship.

Williams is no romantic. She does not make the false claim that the human heart is irresistibly drawn toward democracy, because it is not: the heart is as responsible for fascism and genocide as it is for generosity and justice. Williams claims only that the heart is where we *wrestle with the questions* on which democracy hinges:

> Can we be equitable? Can we be generous? Can we listen with our whole beings, not just our minds, and offer our attention rather than our opinions? And do we have enough resolve in our hearts to act courageously, relentlessly, without giving up—ever—trusting our fellow citizens to join with us in our determined pursuit of a living democracy?

On all of those questions our hearts are conflicted. We want to be equitable and generous. But we also want to cling jealously to our share, even when it is more than we need. We want to listen to others. But afraid of what we might hear, we also look for ways to avoid dialogue with anyone who might disagree with us. We want to trust our fellow citizens. But having been hurt by others, including those close to us, we find it hard to trust strangers. If the human heart is not democracy's first home, it is surely democracy's first forum, where a silent dispute with fateful consequences rumbles on endlessly.

As I make a case for the role of the heart in politics, hard-core political realists may dismiss it as naive when it comes to the rough-and-tumble process of getting elected and governing. I want to meet the realists on their own ground by making a reality claim of my own: anyone who professes to understand politics but dismisses the heart's role in it is either being disingenuous about the leverage gained by manipulating emotions or has not taken a close look at how the world works.

The most casual student of electoral politics knows that the surest way to win votes is to divide and conquer the heart, pitting emotion against intellect. For example, it is a simple fact that the top 1 percent of Americans hold nearly one-quarter of our personal wealth (a concentration of wealth last seen in 1928, just before the Great Depression), while the top 20 percent hold 85 percent of the wealth.[2] However, campaigning on this fact and its economic implications is likely to cost you votes—even among the bottom 80 percent—if your opponent advocates "family, faith, and patriotism." This despite the tragic irony that our families and our confidence in the American dream are being undermined by the rapid shrinkage of America's middle class.

Not only does an appeal to the emotions almost always trump an appeal to intellect, but presenting facts that contradict deeply held beliefs is more likely to reinforce those beliefs than compel people to change them. This defies common sense, of course, but research consistently proves it is true.[3] Show a chart that reveals income inequality to people who have built their lives on the promise of upward mobility, and it is less likely to change their minds than to cause them to call you a socialist or a communist.

If people who dismiss heart talk as irrelevant to politics are not disingenuous, they are simply wrong. They view reality through the distorted lenses of a culture that treats our invisible inner dynamics and our visible behavior as if they belong to different worlds. But inner and outer reality constantly interact, co-creating us and the world in which we live.

What drives the kind of consumerism that helped create our economic crisis except the fear that we do not have enough, even when we do? Or the arrogance that tells us we deserve even more? Or a spiritual emptiness that we try to fill with material goods? And what drives our generosity except an altruistic impulse toward human need? Despite our well-documented material possessiveness, charity is still a hallmark of American life. We are first among the nations in per capita giving: it would take three Frenchmen, seven Germans, or fourteen Italians to equal the charitable donations of one American.[4] The human heart is a force field at least as complex as those known to physicists.

The Heart and Realpolitik

When a person with political influence ignores or denies the heart's power to shape the world—believing, instead, that reason is the prime mover of history—it is a recipe for disaster. On October 23, 2008, Alan Greenspan testified before Congress about the economic meltdown that has led to so much suffering in America and around the world. Greenspan, a leading economist and long-time devotee of the philosopher Ayn Rand who proclaimed the supremacy of reason, served as chairman of the Federal Reserve from 1987 to 2006, an era when our economy was hyped as having an unlimited capacity for growth.

During that time, some of us bought overpriced stocks, houses, or consumer goods we did not need with money we did not have. Our reasons ranged from being conned by the hype or being cheated by liars to out-of-control consumerism or garden-variety greed. When we awoke in the middle of the night worrying about how this high flying could continue, we turned on the television and listened to an endless parade of experts explaining why the law of gravity had been suspended just for us.

Unfortunately, most of those experts failed to mention that our Peter Pan flight into fantasy was a staged illusion supported by very flimsy wires. Then the wires snapped and we crashed. So we turned on the television again as Alan Greenspan testified before members of Congress who seemed to be as confused and distraught as we were. He used the same "rational" economic arguments he had been using for years. But now, through the magic of economics, he arrived at different conclusions.

I caricature this exchange only slightly, drawing on the rights and privileges granted by my dramatic license:

Q: As you look back on this catastrophic wreck involving a train that you and your colleagues had tracked for years with the best tools of economics, what surprises you most?

A: The fact that dishonesty and greed played such a major role in the financial transactions that we allowed the industry to make without any real oversight or regulation.

What Greenspan actually said was that he found himself in "shocked disbelief" to learn that the people who ran unregulated lending institutions had not acted to protect shareholder equity.[5] He had "found a flaw" in his model of "how the world works," a model based on the assumption that people who have power over big money will equate investors' interests with their own and so do not need to be regulated.[6]

With just a few words, Greenspan revealed how blind we become when we ignore the powers of the human heart. If a naval architect designed an ocean liner with a large hole in the hull, leading to the drowning of a thousand souls aboard—and then explained to the Maritime Disaster Board of Inquiry that he had belatedly found a "flaw" in his design—his or her license would be revoked. So why do economists and other experts who routinely factor out the human heart remain among the chief architects of our ship of state?

Given the events of history and the literature that ponders their dynamics—Greek tragedies, the Bible, Shakespeare, and Dostoevsky, to name a few—one might think that the role of the heart as a major driver of all things human would be widely recognized. One might even imagine that failing to reckon the heart's power in fields like economics and politics, or medicine and engineering, for that matter, would be regarded as a sign of rank ignorance.[7]

But many educated Americans who rise to positions of responsibility believe they must operate almost exclusively on the basis of what can be observed and measured because they are educated in a system that mistakenly defines reality that way. And yet, everything human is driven by the invisible powers of the heart. From falling in love with a person who changes the course of your life to distrusting people of a different race, from acts of astonishing courage to the most barbaric of cruelties, from the curiosity that animates science to the fears that paralyze the mind, the human heart is backstage directing the action. Ignore that simple truth, and we put ourselves and our world at risk by missing critical clues about real life.

Once again, I am using the word *heart* to refer to an integral way of knowing, the kind of knowing that allows Terry Tempest Williams to claim that the heart is the place where we embrace democracy's complex and challenging questions. So my case for the heart's pivotal role in human affairs offers no protective cover for the anti-intellectualism that has dogged this country from its earliest days, imperiling democracy at every turn.

When we allow emotions to trump the intellect, we swallow "facts" that are demonstrably untrue, letting them fly around unchallenged in a mockery of civic discourse, supporting public figures who promote fictions to further their own cause. In 2009 and 2010, our vital national debate over health care reform was partially hijacked by a political celebrity's Facebook claim that the administration's proposal would create "death panels" to decide if and when certain infants and elders should die. This is the twenty-first-century equivalent of the "facts" that fueled the Salem witch trials of 1692 and 1693.[8]

Reduce the heart to feelings, and you get politics as a dangerous game of emotional manipulation that can in the long run lead to tyrannies of several sorts. Restore the heart to its rightful role as the integral core of our human capacities, and it gives us a place of power in which to stand, along with the kind of knowledge we need to rebuild democracy's infrastructure from the inside out.

A Farmer's Heart

When we learn to "think with the mind descended into the heart"— integrating cognition and emotion with other faculties like sensation, intuition, and bodily knowledge—the result can be insight, wisdom, and the courage to act on what we know.[9] Here is a story to illustrate the point.

I once led a weekend retreat for twenty elected and appointed officials from Washington, D.C. The men and women who attended bore no resemblance to the public image of bureaucratic hacks. They were committed citizen-leaders who invested long hours of hard work trying to solve vexing social problems. Even more vexing to them, however, were the inner-life issues that had brought them to this retreat.

All of these people had gone into government animated by an ethic of public service, all of them were caught in painful conflicts between their values and power politics, and all of them sought to reclaim the ethic that had animated their desire to serve democracy's cause. For three days, I helped them create a space where they could go deeper than the intellect to the heart-place where all of our faculties converge. For three days they explored their shared dilemma with candor and compassion, seeking creative ways to live in the tension between their heartfelt civic values and the hardball world of politics.

One man in the circle had spent a decade in the Department of Agriculture following twenty-five years of farming in northeastern Iowa. Several times during the retreat, he spoke anxiously about a quandary that awaited him back at his office. He had to decide on a policy related to the preservation of topsoil, a precious natural resource threatened by agribusiness practices that value short-term profits over sustainability, putting the quality of our food supply and the earth's well-being at risk. More than once he said, "My farmer's heart knows what I need to do...." He also knew that following his heart's lead would get him into serious trouble, especially with his superior, who was beholden to agribusiness money.

On Sunday morning, during our final session, the man from Agriculture told us it had become clear to him that he needed to settle the issue in favor of his farmer's heart. After a thoughtful silence, someone asked him, "How will you respond to your boss?"

"It won't be easy," he replied. "But during my time in this circle, I've understood something important. *I don't report to my boss. I report to the land.*"

What this man heard from his heart did not give him practical strategies and tactics to negotiate the complexities that lay ahead. Nonetheless, it gave him solid ground on which to take the next steps. When he got back to his office, he did not change the course of American farming. But because he got access to his heart and did what he could to respond to its imperatives, his actions led to a net moral gain for all concerned. He may have nudged policy toward better stewardship of the earth. He may have inspired some of his colleagues to make their own moral stands. At the very least he now knows that he has an "inner teacher" to consult when his next dilemma shows up.

Think for a moment about the nature of the knowledge held in this "farmer's heart." His emotions were clearly involved; he cared deeply about the land. His caring was interlaced with a wealth of scientific and experiential knowledge drawn from academic research and a quarter-century of farming. He understood the limits and potentials of the land and of the farmer's skillful means, the short- and long-term consequences of various courses of action, and the complex and sometimes contradictory demands that come with a farmer's life.

The man from Agriculture made a decision based on knowledge from diverse sources that interact with and inform each other only at the core of the human self. How did he get to that inward place? By refusing to ignore the tension between his values and the pressures of politics. Instead, he held that tension patiently and reflectively, as only the heart can do, until it broke his heart open to a way forward.

The Power of Heartbreak

As our personal and political lives unfold, the world within us and the world around us continually conflict, collaborate, and give shape to each other. Everything human can be found in the heart as both cause and effect of what happens in the external world. And nothing that happens in the human heart has more power, for better or for worse, than heartbreak.

It was, after all, ordinary Germans—heartbroken by their defeat in World War I and by the economic failures and cultural humiliations that came with the Weimar Republic—who put Hitler in power as he promised to restore their lost sense of "national greatness" through the myth of Aryan supremacy. And it was heartbroken grandmothers of the "disappeared" in Chile and Argentina who brought down murderous tyrants by exposing their cruelty and demanding justice through public demonstrations.

If you have ever loved someone or something—a man, a woman, a child, a job, an idea, or an ideal—you probably know what it means to have your heart broken by failure, loss, betrayal, decline, or death. Like most Americans, I love democracy, and like many I know, it breaks my heart when democracy is threatened, from within or without. What else should I feel when "We the People" find our will trumped by corporate money, official corruption, and Orwellian lies? Or when we undermine ourselves by indulging in cheap animosities toward those who disagree with us instead of engaging our differences like grown-ups?

Diminishments and losses of this sort are among life's painful experiences, and *heartbreak* is the most honest word I know for that pain. But pragmatic Americans have a hard time naming and claiming things of the heart when it comes to public life. Instead of saying "I'm heartbroken" about whatever it is that threatens our version of the American dream—acknowledging our wounds and thus opening them to healing—we withdraw into the silence of private life or express ourselves with the cynicism and anger that make the public realm toxic, producing more psychodrama than social change. To heal the wounds of our body politic, we must understand that these behaviors are the masks heartbreak wears, symptoms rather than the underlying condition.

There are exceptions, of course. Some of the cynicism, anger, and hatred we hear is scripted and strategic. For example, manipulating our ancient fear of "otherness" is a time-tested method to gain power and get wealthy, if you have a public megaphone. Well-known media personalities—and too many political candidates and officeholders—exploit a market that will yield returns as long as fear haunts the human heart, a profitable enterprise in relation to their own financial or political fortunes but one that can bankrupt the commonwealth.

As the norms of social decency weaken, these fearmongers whip up what Henry Giroux has called a "culture of cruelty," working nonstop "to undo democratic values, compassion and any viable notion of justice and its accompanying social relations."[10] When pressed about their inflammatory rhetoric and promotion of stereotypes, they claim that they are patriotic entertainers, not journalists. Their claim might be credible if these media personalities did not work so hard to persuade people that they are reliable sources of political reportage or if they were truly entertaining, as skilled satirists are.

The human experience that these manipulators so skillfully exploit is heartbreak, plain and simple. They use reverse alchemy to turn the gold of human sensibility into the dross of banality, with its potential for evil. Their success reveals what we get when we fail to understand our own heartbreak and do what is required to heal it. Egged on by the hucksters of hate, a handful of citizens becomes violent, slashing the fabric of our common life, while many become cynically or fearfully disengaged, their alienation helping unravel that fabric as they withdraw from the shared task of reweaving it.

What shall we do with our heartbreak so that it yields life, not death? If we were all heartbroken about the same thing, the question would be easy to answer: reach consensus on something better, and join hands toward that end. But the sources of our heartbreak are different and often contradictory: what makes my heart sad may make your heart glad. You may believe that God favors America and blesses the wars we fight or that the virtue of the American economic system is that everyone must be responsible for earning his or her keep. I believe that God has never blessed a nation or a war and that the deepening economic injustice in America contradicts any reasonable conception of a good society.

I name my personal beliefs for the sake of full disclosure, and no more. I will not press those issues here: that kind of argument seldom changes anyone's mind. Instead, I want to explore a more hopeful possibility. Despite our sharp disagreements on the nature of the American dream, many of us on the left, on the right, and in the center have at least this much in common: a shared experience of heartbreak about the condition of our culture, our society, our body politic. That shared heartbreak can build a footbridge of mutual understanding on which we can walk toward each other.

Our sharpest disagreements need not be the seeds of democracy's destruction. If we know how to hold their tensions in ways that open our hearts, they can become proof of democracy's genius and drivers of its renewal.

Two Kinds of Heartbreak Examined

Everyday life is a school of the spirit that offers us chance after chance to practice dealing with heartbreak. Those chances come when we aspire and fail or hope and have our hopes dashed or love and suffer love's loss. If we are able to enter into and consciously engage hard experiences of this sort, our hearts will get the kind of exercise that can make them supple. But if we try to shield ourselves against life's teachable moments, our hearts—like any unexercised muscle—become more vulnerable to stress.

Under stress, an unexercised heart will explode in frustration or fury. If the situation is especially tense, that exploding heart may be hurled like a fragment grenade toward the source of its pain. But a heart that has been consistently exercised through conscious engagement with suffering is more likely to break open instead of apart. Such a heart has learned how to flex to hold tension in a way that expands its capacity for both suffering and joy.

We all know people whose hearts have been broken by the loss of someone or something they loved. Through no fault of their own, they lost homes to a corrupt economy, jobs to inhumane corporate decisions, children to bad youthful choices, friends and family members to violent or untimely death. In the face of such losses, some become bitter and withdrawn. Others become more compassionate, using the insight that comes in the dark and the energy of grief to heal themselves and reach out to others in pain.

The broken-open heart is not a rarity to be found only among saints but a common feature in the lives of ordinary people, including ourselves. You suffer the death of someone who gave your life meaning. Then you go through a long underground passage of grief when life without that person barely seems worth living. But one day you emerge and discover, to your surprise, that *because of* your devastating loss, your heart feels more grateful, alive, and loving. The heart is an alchemical retort that can transform dross into gold.

We will never fully understand why people respond so differently to experiences of heartbreak: there is an eternal mystery about how the shattered soul becomes whole again. But people whose hearts break open, not apart, are usually those who have embraced life's "little deaths" over time, those small losses, failures, and betrayals that can serve as practice runs for the larger deaths yet to come. Some people do this intentionally as a function of their spiritual practice or reflective philosophy of life. Others do it because life takes them to places where it is either "do or die."

We are now at such a place as a nation: we must restore the wholeness of our civic community or watch democracy wither. Hearts opened by the many sources of heartbreak in American life have the potential to help heal our political process. Such hearts are the source of what Lincoln called "our bonds of affection," that sense of unity among strangers that allows us to do what democracy demands of its citizens: engage collectively and creatively with issues of great moment, even—and especially—in times of intense conflict.[11] If we cannot or will not open our hearts to each other, powers that diminish democracy will rush into the void created by the collapse of "We the People." But in the heart's alchemy that community can be restored.

I neither imagine nor yearn for a conflict-free public realm, a fantasy that is tantamount to yearning for a death-free life. Only in a totalitarian society is conflict "banished." Conflict does not disappear, of course, but is merely driven underground, replaced with a public illusion of unity that must be enforced by violence. In a healthy democracy, public conflict is not only inevitable but prized. Taking advantage of our right to disagree fuels our creativity and allows us to adjudicate critical questions of many sorts: true versus false, right versus wrong, just versus unjust.

But when our debates degenerate into throwing fragment grenades, we go well beyond behaving like boors and become barbarians at democracy's gates. We drive from the public square many citizens who do not want a life of combat, citizens who retreat to the illusory safety of their private lives, leaving a public vacuum that antidemocratic powers are eager to fill. When one cannot show up as a citizen without being literally or metaphorically armed, democracy is in decline.

In public or private life, we "arm" ourselves because we want to be invulnerable to heartbreak. Faced with what we perceive as a threat to our emotions, our egos, our values, or our ultimate beliefs, we shut down in hopes of defending ourselves against whatever might breach our defenses. New life arises when we understand that opening ourselves to conflict can expand our capacity to learn, grow, and feel more at home in ourselves and in our world. The odds that conflict will make us larger and more confident instead of smaller and more fearful increase with our willingness to let everyday experience exercise and open our hearts.

Diagnosing Our "Heart Disease"

If we want to support the habits of the heart that make for personal and societal health, we must understand the underlying causes of the "heart disease" that can kill the body politic. Primary among them is inner emptiness, the absence of a strong sense of personal identity, that leaves us vulnerable to false and often toxic systems of "meaning."

Modernity has meant the loss of any semblance of cultural consensus about who we are and what our lives mean. The reassuring voice that once told us, "Here is the answer!" has been replaced by a cacophony of competing voices crying, "Find your personal meaning here!" Of course, freedom to choose our own source of meaning is a pearl of great price, one of democracy's great gifts to us and to the world. And yet it is often gained at the price of becoming isolated, lost, and bereft of value and purpose until we find some way to make sense of our lives.

As we look for that alternative, we have a choice to make: do we turn outward toward one of those clamoring voices, or do we look within? For many of us, the inner is alien territory, unmapped, the last place we want to go. The inner journey that might allow us to find life-giving sources of meaning within us *and* between us is blocked by two fears—that we will get lost in this *terra incognita* and that what we find in those uncharted wastes may frighten or even harm us: "Here be dragons." Fearful of going inward, we become easy prey for the myriad pitchmen of meaning who con us into buying their cut-rate, bogus remedies for emptiness and fear.

A complete inventory of those remedies would fill more pages than I have in this book: they range from surrounding ourselves with mindless distractions to compulsive overwork to alcohol and drug abuse to cultic deference to some guru. I will focus on two false remedies common among us and corrosive of democracy: consumerism and scapegoating. Both distort the relationship between the individual and the civic community, and both point toward the countervailing habits of the heart we must develop if democracy is to thrive.

For many people, consumerism is the drug of choice for assuaging inner emptiness: we purchase goods and services not because we need them but because we think they will shore up our sense of identity and worth. The proof is close at hand in the ads that saturate our public and private lives, ads that rarely focus on the product's utility. Instead, they target the inner needs it allegedly fulfills, informed by market research on what consumers seek. "Want to be youthful, beautiful, sophisticated, or powerful? Buy this!" Our addiction to consumption can run so deep that we keep buying these false promises for the lift they give us, despite the fact that the temporary fix leaves us with emptier pocketbooks and still empty hearts.[12]

Taken to extremes, this kind of consumerism is as toxic to the community as it is to individuals. It does not generate real economic growth and its benefits but creates the illusion of growth and all the pathologies that come in its wake. In the second half of the twentieth century, incomes lagged farther and farther behind the cost of living, and yet many of us insisted on spending as if we still had money. We financed vanity purchases of an overpriced house or overpowered car by playing a rigged credit game with Monopoly money, bringing the economy to the edge of another Great Depression as some of us went over the edge into economic free-fall. Toxic consumerism has pushed many Americans—including those who tried to live within their means—out of jobs they once held and homes they once owned. And that, in turn, has created problems ranging from clinical depression to the breakdown of families and communities.

If the recession continues to create high unemployment (over 9 percent nationally as I write, and over 40 percent among some subgroups), it does not bode well for our capacity to embrace democracy's diversity and the tensions it brings. In "How a New Jobless Era Will Transform America," Don Peck outlines the case made by the economic historian

Benjamin Friedman in his book *The Moral Consequences of Economic Growth:*

> Lengthy periods of economic stagnation or decline have almost always left society more mean-spirited and less inclusive, and have usually stopped or reversed the advance of rights and freedoms. A high level of national wealth, Friedman writes, "is no bar to a society's retreat into rigidity and intolerance once enough of its citizens lose the sense that they are getting ahead." When material progress falters . . . people become more jealous of their status relative to others. Anti-immigrant sentiment typically increases, as does conflict between races and classes; concern for the poor tends to decline.[13]

Among those Americans who live above the poverty line, some have learned the ancient lesson that "less is more." They have cut back their purchasing to cover basic needs instead of indulging nonessential wants. They have discovered the values of reusing, repairing, and sharing material things, as well as nonmaterial values such as investing more time and energy in creating mutually supportive relationships with family, friends, and neighbors. As one guide to life in hard times puts it, "Keep in mind that security and satisfaction are more easily acquired from friends than from money."[14]

We need more and more people who understand such simple truths. To embrace the economic myth of "endless growth" or the personal myth that material possessions create meaning is to embrace illusions that portend political as well as personal calamity. Why become serious about citizenship—a role that requires long-term commitment and rarely yields quick results—when consumerism's "instant gratifications" are close at hand? Our obsession with consumption becomes one more driver of our exodus from the public arena, one more force that saps our collective power to act as "We the People."

A second "cure" for our inner emptiness is scapegoating, a remedy with consequences for the individual and the community that are even more deadly than unbridled consumerism. As Benjamin Friedman suggests, some find solace in blaming their problems on the alien "other," a pathology documented almost daily in the news. We project our inner shadows on people of a different race, social class, religion, or ideology and blame them for whatever is lacking in our lives. We restore our sense of identity by tearing others' down, claiming our "superiority" against the backdrop of their "inferiority."

This form of "heart disease" is not as common as consumerism, but what it lacks in frequency it makes up for in virulence. Taken to extremes, scapegoating feeds the political pathology called fascism, a movement ideology centered on a "radical and authoritarian nationalism" that actively suppresses "openness and opposition" to the movement and the nation-state it hopes to commandeer.[15] When this diseased brand of nationalism rushes in to fill our inner emptiness, its mildest manifestation is the belief that nation's critics are unpatriotic, even traitorous. At its worst, it breeds ideologies parallel to the madness of Nazism, constellating collective evil of the sort that powered the Holocaust.

Even when scapegoating does not go to fascist extremes, acting on our fear of "the other" threatens democracy. Some people feel secure only by withdrawing from the public realm into a protected private life with people of "their own kind." Examples range from people who must live in gated or guarded communities to those who never venture beyond the "tunnel" they travel regularly between family, work, religious community, and friends. A sheltered life may help empty and isolated people find something that passes for meaning, community, and security. But "communities" that live behind gated walls or in bunkers connected by a tunnel are bogus versions of the real thing. If they do not actively destroy democracy, they are a profound drag on its well-being.

Of course, many Americans find it not only possible but actually pleasant to live among strangers and take a pass on scapegoating. Put simply, these are the grown-ups who left the adolescent mind-set behind and learned to take responsibility for their own inner struggles for meaning instead of seeking someone to blame. And when their struggles are outward rather than inward—as when some very real injustice diminishes their lives—they know how to take creative action in an effort to set things right instead of hunkering down in hatred against an imaginary enemy. These Americans have the habits of the heart that a democracy requires.

The Self a Democracy Needs

When a democratic society is working as it should—calling people to individual freedom and collective responsibility—it helps shape the kind of self that perpetuates democracy, a self that is simultaneously independent and interdependent.

Democracy needs and, at its best, breeds people who have minds of their own. Individual entrepreneurship and personal creativity have given rise to advances in everything from business to technology to the arts. Independent thinking can also help get the ship of state back on course when ideological conformism leads us astray. And yet anyone who does not understand that the self is interdependent with others does not understand what it takes to be entrepreneurial, creative, and political, let alone what it means to be human.

"It takes a village" to do many things: raise a child, test our ideas in dialogue, gather the resources required to translate a concept into reality, find stimulation and support for even the most solitary forms of creative endeavor. Ask a group of people who have succeeded at anything—from achieving prominence in worthy endeavors to surviving hard times—how many of them believe that their survival or success is due in part to others. The few who fail to raise their hands are almost sure to be lost in delusions of adequacy.

The kind of self that democracy needs is no stranger to inner emptiness or fear. And yet such a self does not seek identity and meaning in the illusions of consumerism, the evasions of scapegoating, or any other false remedy. The healthy self finds an identity that allows it to feel at home in its own skin *and* in the company of others, even (and sometimes especially) "alien" others. The healthy self stands on its own two feet and understands the many ways in which it depends on and must contribute to the community.

Such a self does not happen by accident. It takes shape only when a society is rich with opportunities for citizens to reflect on and direct the dynamics of their hearts. In the next four chapters, I explore several settings in which those dynamics are formed. Chapter IV focuses on our large-scale institutions of government; Chapter V, on the open and free-wheeling public life that democracy requires; Chapter VI, on local institutions such as public schools and religious institutions; and Chapter VII, on a variety of settings, from physical to virtual, that I call "safe space for deep democracy."

Together these venues comprise the *visible* infrastructure of democracy that creates and contains energies that shape the *invisible* infrastructure called habits of the heart. What must we do in the venues of our common life to generate the habits that will keep democracy alive and allow it to thrive? That is the question to which I now turn.

[C H A P T E R IV]

The Loom of Democracy

It is easy enough to see that all through our lives we are faced with the task of reconciling opposites which, in logical thought, cannot be reconciled. The typical problems of life are insoluble on the level of being on which we normally find ourselves. How can one reconcile the demands of freedom and discipline in education? Countless mothers and teachers, in fact, do it, but no one can write down a solution. They do it by bringing into the situation a force that belongs to a higher level where opposites are transcended—the power of love.

—E. F. SCHUMACHER, *Small Is Beautiful*[1]

As the British economist E. F. Schumacher wrote those words— musing on the way "countless mothers and teachers" reconcile opposites like freedom and discipline while educating a child—I doubt that he was thinking about Abraham Lincoln's first inaugural address or the governing structures created by America's founders. Nonetheless, Schumacher's insight into our capacity to resolve "divergent problems" illuminates the genius of Lincoln's presidency and of our democratic institutions.

Lincoln's first inaugural was addressed to an America on the brink of a civil war. He concluded by saying, "We are not enemies, but friends" and appealing to "the better angels of our nature" to help us restore "the bonds of our affection." When Schumacher says that divergent problems can be reconciled only through the power of love, he speaks a language that Lincoln would have understood.

America's founders would also have understood Schumacher's words, but for a different reason. Wanting to improve on the repressive governments of Old Europe, they needed to create political structures strong enough to hold the tension of divergent problems. The democratic institutions they invented were designed to function like a loom, holding the tension of our political disagreements to keep us talking with each other and giving us chance after chance to reweave the fabric of our common life.[2] At the heart of the American experiment is an insight akin to Schumacher's about what it takes to educate a child: a good society will emerge from the tension between freedom and discipline, between what the Constitution calls "the blessings of liberty" and the rule of law.

Of course, the challenge of holding a child in the tension between freedom and discipline is hardly comparable to Lincoln's challenge of holding the Union together or the founders' challenge of creating institutions capable of holding democracy's endless dilemmas. Still, all of these are divergent problems, the kind whose best outcomes are achieved not with either-or but with both-and solutions, a principle that is as applicable to "doing democracy" as it is raising a child.

In Lincoln's last public address—delivered two days after Lee surrendered to Grant—the president spoke of the South in a spirit of reconciliation that transcended war's either-or logic in which a triumphant winner lords it over a humiliated loser. Speaking to a crowd of Union loyalists who remained "fixed on the question [of] whether the seceded States, so called, are in the Union or out of it," Lincoln refused to accept the divergent terms of the question itself.

Instead, he framed the issue in the reconciling language of the heart, saying of the defeated Confederates, "Finding themselves safely at home, it would be utterly immaterial whether they had ever been abroad."[3] If he yielded to Northern demands that he declare the South to have been out of the Union, Lincoln argued, it would "have no effect other than the mischievous one of dividing our friends."[4]

A reporter named Noah Brooks was in the crowd that gathered on the White House lawn to hear what was to be Lincoln's last speech; the president was assassinated three days later. In Brooks's dispatch about the speech, he wrote that Lincoln set forth "the generous policy which should be pursued toward the South," followed by this aside: "That this was not the sort of speech which the multitude had expected is tolerably certain."[5] What they heard instead was Lincoln speaking in the reconciling voice of the better angels of our nature, a voice that represents the human heart and American democracy at their best.

Learning to Hold Tension Creatively

Our private lives abound with either-or problems that are best resolved with a both-and response. We raise children and teach students who need both freedom and discipline. We have significant relationships with a partner or friend in which the needs of both parties must be honored no matter how contradictory they may be. We hold jobs we must keep in order to stay afloat while finding a way to lift our own spirits against the downward pull of the work we do. We have aspirations we know we will never achieve that still keep calling to us.

Dilemmas of this sort do not yield to conventional logic. Nonetheless, we learn to embrace their tensions in ways that open us to something new—and in that fact lies hope that we can learn to hold democracy's divergent problems. Aided by the power of love, we help a child learn and grow; we find mutual satisfaction in correlating our needs with those of another person; we learn how to keep our spirits alive, on and off the job; we let our impossible aspirations keep drawing us toward the next possibility.

How, exactly, do we resolve dilemmas that tempt us to choose either this or that and instead hold the tension long enough to let a "third thing" emerge? According to Schumacher:

> Divergent problems . . . *demand*, and thus provoke the *supply* of,
> forces from a higher level, thus bringing love, beauty, goodness, and
> truth into our lives. It is only with the help of these higher forces that
> the opposites can be reconciled in the living situation.[6]

Supply and demand is a law of economics, of course, and Schumacher suggests that our hearts respond to some version of this law. Everyday life brings divergent *demands* of many sorts. These "provoke" our abundant inner *supplies* of "love, beauty, goodness, and truth," powers that can transform tension from a destructive force into creative energy—if we hold the tension long enough to let it open our hearts so they can work their alchemy.

Schumacher's analysis is astute: the heart's transformative powers will be released only if we are willing to make ourselves vulnerable to urgent demands for them. And yet it is also potentially misleading. The heart has the *capacity* to turn tension toward constructive ends, but there is nothing automatic about it. The powers we need will be released only if the heart has been made supple by practice so that it breaks open instead of apart under stress. And that is a very big *if*.

When the heart breaks apart, our "lesser angels" are set loose, forces whose destructive handiwork is on display everywhere we look. When those dark powers are unleashed, the divergent problems we face may lead us to explode at a partner or a child, meeting our needs but not theirs, or to sink into cynicism at work, resigning ourselves to a life of resentment, or to become addicted to one of the many anesthetics available to dull the pain of our personal limitations.

Will the heart break open or apart when it encounters life's demands? Everything depends on the qualities of the heart on which those demands are laid and on how it has been formed or deformed. Is it an experienced heart, a reflective heart, a heart made supple by inner exercise and responsive engagement with life? Or is it a heart grown brittle from being wounded, unattended and unhealed, sheltered and withdrawn, a heart more prone to shattering in the face of yet another demand?

As we who are parents, for example, try to give a child both freedom and discipline, we may run into inner obstacles that keep us from holding that polarity with grace. Perhaps we are overwhelmed by fear about the future of the child we love. Driven by anxiety, we may tilt the balance toward confinement and safety instead of freedom and its risks, depriving our child of the growth that can only come from learning the hard way. Or perhaps we look back on our own childhood as repressive, making our movement into adulthood slower and more painful than it needed to be. Driven by resentment, we may tilt the balance toward more freedom than our child can handle.

If we are wise, we will do inner work to overcome obstacles of that sort. Every teacher of the inner life, spiritual or secular—from Ralph Waldo Emerson to Howard Thurman, from Zalman Schachter to the Dalai Lama—recommends some form of practice or "exercise" to help the heart flex enough to break open instead of shattering. Mindfulness, meditation or prayer, reading great literature about the human condition, spending time in solitude and silence, talking with a counselor or spiritual guide—practices of that sort can help us open our hearts before fear or resentment overcomes us and we do unintended harm. If we are not wise enough to prepare ourselves for those moments when we need open hearts, the harm we do may compel us to go within, giving *us* a chance to learn the hard way how important it is to exercise hearts.

And how, exactly, do we open our hearts to reconcile divergent problems? As Schumacher rightly says, "no one can write down a solution." But we *can* name, as I did at the end of Chapter II, the habits of the heart we must exercise if we are to use the tension of divergent problems toward creative ends in our political life. Once we have named specific habits, we can explore ways to teach and learn them in the various settings of our lives.

The largest and most comprehensive of those settings is American democracy itself, the complex of structures and processes designed by the founders to hold the tension of divergent problems on a massive scale. In order to make use of that force field to cultivate democratic habits of the heart, we must understand what it demands of us *and* what it can evoke from us if we embrace its demands. In service of that goal, I want to say more about how the "loom of democracy" works.

The Endless Argument

Political life in a democracy is a nonstop flow of contradictions and conflicts. What shall we do when the will of the majority infringes on the rights of a minority? If we want both freedom and justice, what is the proper balance of unrestrained personal or economic activity and government regulation? Which is most effective in transforming various kinds of behaviors: education, incentives, or legal sanctions? In the face of a foreign threat, is our national interest more likely to be secured through quiet diplomacy or saber-rattling?

In the face of divergent problems like these, what kinds of institutions will allow people who disagree to open up and work together rather than shut down and turn against each other? When America's founders wrestled with that question, they were motivated in part by a desire to grow beyond Old World traditions of "resolving" conflicts by royal decree. But their more immediate motivation was the need to deal with the serious conflicts *among themselves*. The fact that the founders were all white, male landholders did not make for a united approach to declaring independence from British rule and framing a national constitution. Far from it. Their own diversity of convictions compelled them to invent political institutions capable of surviving conflict and of putting it to good use.

The institutions they created can be seen most clearly through Schumacher's lens of "divergent problems" that "demand, and thus provoke the supply of, forces from a higher level." I do not mean that the founders created institutions that bring divine beings to our aid, a notion that is supported by precisely zero evidence. What they created is a form of government that maintains tension over time rather than rushing to resolve it prematurely and falsely, thus provoking a supply of human creativity that is never achieved when problems are resolved by fiat.

In the insightful and incisive words of the historian Joseph Ellis, the governing institutions the founders bequeathed us were "not about providing answers" but about "providing a framework in which the salient questions could continue to be debated."[7] Our form of government was designed not to suppress our differences but to keep the energy of their tension alive so that it could animate the body politic. Evidence of that fact is found in all the key structures and processes of American democracy:

- The federal separation of powers and the system of checks and balances that holds issues in tension between the administrative, legislative, and judicial branches of the government, keeping them alive in short- and long-term cycles
- The ongoing tension between federal and state authorities, a dynamic in which the rights and responsibilities of both levels of government are constantly being sorted out[8]
- Our adversarial system of justice in which the tensions between attorneys representing the plaintiff and the defense are held by a judge who represents the rule of law and by the deliberations of a jury
- Virtually every constitutional amendment in the Bill of Rights, which was written to limit the powers of the federal government and maintain the tensions that keep a democracy healthy
- The regular cycle of elections, which invites political opponents to compete by drawing voters into the tension of debate and allowing them to settle an issue—knowing that there will continue to be critics of the winning position and that another election is not too far down the road[9]

With provisions of this sort, the founders hoped to avoid the wreckage that litters human history, the wreckage caused by "resolving" conflict with violence. Forced resolutions are false resolutions: repression merely drives dissent underground, where sooner or later it explodes, leaving new violence in its wake. In American-style democracy, the incessant conflicts of political life are meant to be contained within a dialectic of give-and-take, generating and even necessitating collaboration and inventiveness. These principles create a political system that can and does try our souls. It frustrates, maddens, exhausts, and appalls us when big problems go unsolved because we cannot muster enough agreement to solve them or when problems we thought we had put to rest are called back into play.

And yet this is one of the most crucial lessons of the twentieth century, one that we forget at our peril: tension is a sign of life, and the end of tension is a sign of death. "The Final Solution" (*die Endlösung*) was the name given by the Germans to the reign of death we know as the Holocaust. Germany—weakened by war, economic collapse, and multiple social crises—had suffered a profound blow to its national pride. The Nazis gained absolute power by playing on the public's collective broken heart, creating a demonic mythology of Aryan supremacy. Hitler, a master at manipulating hearts that were broken apart, not open, released the collective shadow within the German psyche. The Jews, with their long history of being scapegoated, were close at hand, and so was the Final Solution. If the end of tension is what you want, fascism is the thing for you. But understand that the day we decide on a "final solution" to our problems is the day much begins to die—perhaps including, as many have cautioned, you or me and "our kind."

The United States Constitution is a life-giving set of principles and practices in part because it makes final solutions impossible. As Joseph Ellis argues, it is "a novel political discovery" that defies "logic and the accumulated wisdom of the entire European political tradition" because "the Constitution, like history itself, [is designed to sustain] an argument without end." Embedded in the Constitution, says Ellis, is "an ongoing negotiation" in which all resolutions are tentative and no one part of the government holds the power to decide. This "deliberate blurring of sovereignty" is not "a fatal weakness" but "an abiding strength." The genius of the Constitution is that it enshrines "an argumentative process in which no such thing as a last word would ever be uttered."[10]

Of course, the founders had more in mind than argument for the sake of argument, as the case of George Washington illustrates. Originally, he had wanted the balance of power to tip more decisively toward the federal government for the sake of centralized control. But Washington came to see that the tension of the debate that led to the Constitution—the kind of tension the Constitution was designed to maintain in perpetuity—had called forth, in his own words, "abilities which would otherwise not perhaps [have] been exerted that have thrown new lights upon the science of government, that have given the rights of man a full and fair discussion."[11]

Washington's point is easily generalized. A political system that allows us to keep working on collective solutions to vexing problems but refuses to take any question off the table permanently calls forth creative capacities that lie dormant under autocratic rule. If we are willing and able to hold the tensions that American democracy deliberately creates, the system itself will help us develop the habits of heart required for the health of the body politic.

The Endless Challenge

In the democracy crafted by the founders, the most recent solution to a problem does not remove that problem from our national agenda. Sooner or later, someone calls for a different solution, and we continue to work away at problems so complex that they cannot be resolved with a final stroke of the pen. Democratic institutions, when working as they should, compel us to hold the tension of "salient questions" and stay open to the next answer, and the next, and the next—sometimes for the better, sometimes for the worse—often enough to keep democracy's promise alive.

How else can we understand, for example, America's long, painful, and ongoing struggle for racial justice? From the beginning, we have held the tension between the founders' declaration that "all men are created equal" and the most rabid forms of racism. It is a tension that has made the American dream a nightmare for too many for too long. But because we have continued to hold it, we have slowly opened to something new and sometimes better.

Step by painful step, we left slavery behind, granted full status (in theory) to those whom our Constitution had counted as three-fifths of a human being, dealt with the subversive setback known as Jim Crow, gave African American citizens the same civil rights enjoyed by other Americans, and became a nation capable of electing an African American president. We have done all of this with unforgivable slowness, and in recent decades, we have even turned the clock back. As the legal scholar Michelle Alexander has demonstrated, African Americans now live under "the new Jim Crow," which can only be overthrown by a popular movement protesting the unjust laws that have made it so.[12]

And yet what progress would America have made on any significant issue if we did not have political institutions capable of holding tension creatively? For a partial answer, look at the many authoritarian states where popular uprisings for something better are brutally suppressed before a new vision can take hold. Progress in America has often come from the agitation of ordinary people, heartbroken people, who would not settle for the status quo. It was people power, not the wisdom of our leaders, that compelled Congress to pass the Civil Rights Act of 1964 and the Voting Rights Act of 1965.[13] That kind of change requires an institutional loom strong enough to hold the tension of popular agitation, allowing pass after pass of the shuttle in the endless effort to weave and reweave the fabric of a common life.

We are imperfect people living in an imperfect world, so we will hold the tension of racial injustice as long as the nation lasts. If we remain a democracy, we will be compelled to let that tension open our hearts to the next best response, time and time again, trying to move an ever-ignoble reality closer to the nobility of the vision on which we were founded by men as imperfect as we. The founders could not have imagined the diversity that characterizes America today, let alone the spread of voting rights to groups they dismissed. And yet the intensity of their own disagreements helped them understand that harnessing the energy of conflict on behalf of creativity, not destruction, had to become a fundamental feature of American politics, and they designed governing structures with that in mind.

Democracy is threatened by anything that undermines the tension-holding capacity of our "loom of government." That threat arises, for example, when one of the three branches of government circumvents another—as when the executive trumps Congress in declaring war—thus weakening the system of checks and balances. It arises when presidential "signing statements" are issued, which have the effect of modifying "duly enacted laws" outside of the legislative process and without public knowledge. It arises again when big money dominates the political process, creating a shadow government and obscuring the true play of power in our land.

As I was writing this chapter, I came across three more stories that highlight how easily the tension-holding function of the loom of democracy can be compromised. The first told about well-heeled lobbies that pay homeless people to clean up, dress up, and stand in line all night so they can fill the seats at congressional hearings where that lobby's interests are on the line. This, of course, prevents people opposed to the lobby's agenda from sitting in on the hearing.[14]

The second story focused on a senior senator who rose to power by fighting campaign finance reform, "protecting the rights" of big money as a form of freedom of speech. Early in his Senate career, he discovered that "he could mount filibusters against routine procedural motions required before House-Senate legislative negotiations could begin," thus effectively "running out the clock" on a campaign finance overhaul that he proceeded to fight for years. "It dawned on me," said the senator, "that it is pretty important and certainly useful to learn as much about the procedure as you can, because frequently procedure is policy."[15] The senator failed to mention that the tactic he perfected subverts the founders' intention that we hold our tensions in open democratic debate.

The third story documents the way our justice system is being undermined as judges, prosecutors, and defense attorneys collude "in practices that render the courtroom efficient but unjust," breaking down "the internal checks and balances within the legal process." Under the guise of unclogging our courts in order to expedite justice, "prosecutors abuse their discretion by ignoring difficult cases," "judges become prosecutors, pressing impoverished defendants into unwarranted plea bargains," and "public defenders ignore evidence that might clear their hapless clients."[16]

There is no end to the ways that clever or powerful people can compromise the tension-holding function of democracy. For those of us who care about such things, the question is clear: will we allow such people to help bring down democracy? Or will we use the moral tension that their subversion creates in us to energize more active forms of citizenship, advancing the cause of civilization as we go?

Beyond Fight or Flight

If "advancing the cause of civilization" seems a bit overdone, consider this: the ancient project called "becoming civilized" has been shaped to a surprising extent by our species' need to create life-giving approaches to holding tension. Looked at in these terms, American democracy is the crowning political achievement of humankind's long march toward trying to subdue the barbarians. If democracy fails, we not only lose what Winston Churchill called "the worst form of government except all the others that have been tried." We also reverse the course of cultural evolution.

Human beings arrive in this world with a "fight or flight" response hardwired into the sympathetic nervous system. When we perceive a threat, real or imagined, our instant impulse is to strike back or run away. This ancient instinct to resolve the tension created by a threat *right now* is useful when we are about to be attacked by a wooly mammoth, mugged by a slightly more evolved mammal, or flattened by a bus. But when we are captive to our hardwiring, we take that instinct with us into situations where it can double our trouble, situations where there are wiser ways to respond.

In the grip of the fight or flight response, we fail to distinguish between threats that truly endanger us and experiences that merely take us out of our comfort zone. We also fail to understand that some apparent resolutions of conflict are false: they create only momentary surcease, followed by the multiplication of tensions. Our fondness for false resolutions explains why tranquilizers sell so well, why groups trying to make a decision often tolerate debate only briefly before calling for an up-or-down vote, why the intrusion of someone who is "not from around here" may cause us alarm, and why some of us believe that we must eliminate our "enemies" rather than listen to and talk with them.

Part of becoming civilized is learning that the tension temporarily relieved by a tranquilizer might, in fact, be a call to change some aspect of one's life. Or that a debate sustained over time might lead to a better solution of the problem. Or that the "alien other" might be a bearer of important information, even good news. Or that we might be safer as a people if our response to our "enemies" were less macho and more measured. If we are willing to hold tensions like these with patience, we will get better resolutions of dilemmas at every level of life.

So early in the project called civilization, we began devising cultural inventions to free ourselves from the tyranny of our hardwiring by finding ways to develop other faculties—intellect, intuition, feeling, imagination, will—which, taken together, constitute that core of self-hood called the human heart. This still unfinished project is driven by the knowledge that we can and must transcend the fight or flight response. Why? Because the reflex that defends us against dangers also prevents us from learning and growing when it becomes our default response to whatever threatens our personal status quo. Worse yet, the fight or flight reflex leads to a geometric multiplication of violence that will eventually take all of us down.

Language was one of the first inventions that helped us convert tension into life-giving energy. As it became possible to respond to apparent threats verbally instead of physically, we were no longer limited to striking out at the source of our fear or fleeing from it in terror. Now we could ask it, in effect, to identify itself and declare its intentions. With a simple "Hey! What's going on here?" we can try to determine if it is an active threat or a happy surprise that might have something to teach us. And if it turns out to be a real threat, language may give us a chance to buy time for negotiating a peace before we go to war.

The importance of language in loosening the grip of the fight or flight response gives us all the more reason to reject the demagogic rhetoric so prominent in our political discourse today, rhetoric tailor-made to trigger the sympathetic nervous system. When we speak words of that sort or give them an audience, we reverse the long process of "becoming civilized" and nullify one of humankind's hardest-won victories.

Art is a second invention that helps us overcome the fight or flight response. A good poem, painting, novel, drama, or musical composition is animated by tension held creatively, making our experience of it a heart- and mind-stretching encounter. As we enter into a true work of art, it enters into us, giving us a visceral experience of the animating potentials of tension.

A painting is more likely to engage the viewer when it contains some degree of tension involving contrasts of light and dark, coolness and warmth, or movement and stillness. A novel is boring unless its characters have contradictions within and between themselves and its plot unfolds in a manner that creates tension about where the action might go. In poetry, too, tension plays a vital role. As the poet and critic Allen Tate wrote in reference to certain technical aspects of language, "Many poems that we . . . think of as good poetry . . . have certain common features that will allow us to invent, for their sharper apprehension, the name of a single quality. I shall call that quality tension."[17]

The same principle applies to theater, as poignantly illustrated by the comments of "Basim," an Iraqi playwright whose safety requires that he write under a pseudonym. Basim wrote about Iraqis who served as interpreters for the U.S. Army because they believed in the American agenda of liberation. They and their families quickly became prime targets for assassination and were protected as "assets" by the American military as long as their services were required. But as the American strategy in Iraq changed, we stopped protecting our collaborators, forcing them either to risk staying in their homeland or go into exile. "For at least ninety minutes," said Basim, "I want the audience to experience the tension in which people like this are now living."[18]

That, in a nutshell, is the civilizing impulse behind the arts: holding tension in aesthetic forms that open us to an empathetic encounter with the stranger, or the strange, that can reveal what we have in common, generate new possibilities in our minds and hearts, and turn otherness from a source of fear into a source of growth. Art of any excellence models creative tension-holding, offering an experience that can help us see, understand, and embrace the tensions of our own lives.

Religion is a third cultural development intended to help us hold tension more creatively than the fight or flight instinct allows. That may sound like a stretch given the widespread impression that religion has produced distrust, animosity, and war more often than peace. And yet in every case I know where religion has borne bitter fruit, the true faith of one or more traditions has been distorted by fanatics or manipulated by cynics whose agendas were not religious but political, people who were often nonbelievers. The true intent of all the great world religions is to help people find meaning and purpose amid life's endless tensions—especially the tension involved in trying to live a meaningful life despite the certainty of death, which would seem to obliterate all meaning.

Christians, for example, have asked, "What does it mean to live in between the mythical Garden of Eden, before evil came into the world, and the mythical New Jerusalem, where all will be well once again?" What does it mean, that is, to live meaningfully in the midst of human history, surrounded by endless suffering? It is easy to find examples of religion being manipulated to amplify rather than transcend our tensions. But it is easier by far to find examples of ordinary people who draw on religion's deep well for the courage to live faithfully amid distressing contradictions.

A fourth civilizing invention is *education.* A good education teaches us to hold contradictions reflectively rather than reactively, a habit of the heart that lies behind all social, cultural, and scientific breakthroughs. The civilizing impact of science, for example, does not come primarily from its most widely heralded discoveries. It comes from insisting that we embrace contradictory observations and explanations, using the experimental method to let their tensions advance our knowledge. Good scientists do not fear divergent views but welcome them for whatever new truth they may reveal. They also know that every new truth is likely to be followed, sooner or later, by yet another contradiction and that only by holding such tensions over time can we advance our knowledge.

Long before modern science became education's dominant paradigm, there was the medieval curriculum called the *trivium* (grammar, logic, and rhetoric) and the *quadrivium* (arithmetic, geometry, music, and astronomy). These programs are the immediate ancestors of our "liberal arts," so named because they offer the knowledge necessary to live as free (Latin *liber*) men or women.[19] Knowledge of this sort is liberating not only because it steeps us in the wisdom of the past; it also accustoms us to ambiguity and paradox, preparing us to find our way into an unpredictable future. A liberal education helps us embrace diverse ideas without becoming paralyzed in thought or action. It teaches us how to claim our own voices in the midst of the clamorous crowd, staying engaged with the communal conversation of a democracy in ways that keep opening us to larger versions of truth.

Democracy and Self-Transcendence

Democracy itself is the fifth cultural creation that helps us transcend the fight or flight response—which brings us back to where we began this ten-minute tour of the evolution of civilization. But democracy is not just one more item to be added to this list. It is a political process for creating a common life that builds on millennia of human attempts to transcend our fight or flight reflex. The tension-holding structures of a democracy allow the best of our leaders to speak meaningfully against reflexive decisions, as Abraham Lincoln did in his first inaugural address on the eve of the Civil War. Referring to the pending issues of slavery and secession, Lincoln said:

> My countrymen, . . . think calmly and well upon this whole subject.
> Nothing valuable can be lost by taking time. If there be an object
> to hurry any of you, in hot haste, to a step which you would never
> take deliberately, that object will be frustrated by taking time; but no
> good object can be frustrated by it.[20]

Like language, the arts, religion, and education, democracy does not propose to bring life's tensions to an end. Instead, it offers us a process for using them creatively, providing political structures that promise to turn the energy of tension toward constructive ends. Because it holds out that promise, life in a democracy can trigger a "tend and befriend" response that some biologists believe to be as deep-seated within us as the fight or flight instinct. One of them writes that the "dominant metaphor" among people who study the biology of stress "represents the threatening social landscape as a solitary kill-or-be-killed world. My work suggests instead that the human response to stress is characterized at least as much by tending to and befriending others."[21]

Alexis de Tocqueville clearly saw that some of democracy's key features encourage and strengthen this relational, associational instinct to a degree unknown under Old World tyrannies. As the biographer Leo Damrosch notes, Tocqueville looked at American life from the standpoint of one who came from a nation where the "law prohibited any assembly of more than twenty people unless they had obtained official permission."[22]

So Tocqueville was especially struck by the vigor of associational life in America, as this passage from *Democracy in America* demonstrates:

> No sooner do you set foot on American soil than you find yourself
> in a sort of tumult. A confused clamor rises up on all sides, and a
> thousand voices reach your ears, each expressing some social need.
> Everything is in motion around you. The people of one district

have come together to decide whether to build a church; in another
they're working to elect a representative. Farther off, delegates from
the countryside are hurrying into town to advise on certain local
improvements; in another village the farmers have left their fields
to debate plans for a road or a school. Some citizens assemble for the
sole purpose of declaring their disapproval of the government's poli-
cies, while others proclaim that the men holding office are fathers of
their country.[23]

In France, as Damrosch notes, "most of these measures would have
been dictated from above, and the rest would have been forbidden."
Then Damrosch quotes Tocqueville again: "Democracy doesn't give
people the most competent government, but it does what the most
competent government is often powerless to do. It spreads throughout
the entire social body a restless activity, a superabundant strength,
an energy that never exists without it."[24] Behind all of this activity
are habits of the heart formed and practiced in part simply because
democracy makes it *possible* to do so. The need for association is one of
the deepest needs of the human heart, and it will always out if given
half a chance.

Still, Tocqueville was not starry-eyed about the long-term prospects
of America's associational vigor. He prophesied dark possibilities, even
inevitabilities, as he looked toward a day when the decentralized
agrarian society of nineteenth-century America would be overwhelmed
by industrialization and the centralization of power that would come
with it. Nearly two centuries ago he wrote:

> It is easy to foresee the time when men will be less and less able to
> produce, by themselves, the commonest necessities of life. The task of
> the social power will therefore increase endlessly, and its very efforts
> will make that task bigger every day. The more it takes the place of
> associations, the more individuals will lose the idea of associating and
> will need its assistance. These causes and effects engender each other
> without end.[25]

Today we are living out this powerful cycle of cause and effect: the more we depend on massive forms of "social power," political and economic, the less we depend on one another. Look around right now at all of the things you regard as essential to your well-being that were not produced by you or your friends and neighbors, nor could they have been. Few of us would volunteer to live without these things. But the less we depend on each other, the more we weaken the interdependence that helps us develop democratic habits of the heart. And the less interdependent we are, the more likely we are to become people among whom consumerism trumps citizenship.

At one point in *Democracy in America,* Tocqueville writes about the social conditions under which despotism arises. He describes with astonishing accuracy the privatized individual we see all around us today, whose world has become so small that he or she cannot assist in weaving a common life:

> Each [such person], living apart, is as a stranger to the fate of all the rest; his children and his private friends constitute to him the whole of mankind. As for the rest of his fellow citizens, he is close to them, but he does not see them; he touches them, but he does not feel them; he exists only in himself and for himself alone; and if his kindred still remain to him, he may be said at any rate to have lost his country.[26]

Read in the twenty-first-century context of an increasingly privatized America, Tocqueville's words are prescient and unsettling. The privatization of life that has come with our growing dependence on centralized power, economic as well as political, makes it all the more urgent that we do what we can to develop democratic habits of the heart in every setting available to us.

How we might do so is the question to which I turn in the next three chapters. I look first at ways we can preserve and enrich the public life, a complex of settings essential to democracy and available to us on a daily basis, an arena in which "We the People" moves beyond mere words to become an embodied experience.

[C H A P T E R V]

Life in the Company of Strangers

There is a community of the spirit.
Join it, and feel the delight
of walking in the noisy street,
and being the noise.

—RUMI, "A Community of the Spirit"[1]

Years ago, during a terrifying ride up Broadway, a New York City taxi driver gave me two lasting gifts: the most evocative description of public life I know and a vivid example of how living "in the company of strangers" can help us develop and exercise democratic habits of the heart.

As we careened uptown at a dangerous clip, I asked the cabbie how he liked his job. I thought he might drive more cautiously if I reminded him that he had not just a job but a life. My mistake. Apparently my driver had been waiting a long time for someone to ask this very question. He responded with great enthusiasm, turning and gesturing as he talked, often driving no-handed. The ride became more perilous, but what he said made the risk worth taking:

Well, you never know who's getting into the cab, so it's a little dangerous. But you meet a lot of people. You get to know *the public*. Which teaches you a lot in life. You don't know anything if you don't know the public. You exchange ideas and you learn a lot from people. It's like going to school. Meeting all these different kinds of people, everything helps, it doesn't hurt. If you only like one kind of people, it's no good! We talk, if I have a better idea, I tell 'em! Maybe they say yes, maybe they say no—that's how I educate myself. It makes me happy. You can't buy this kind of education. If you're with the same kind of people all the time, it's like wearing the same suit all the time—you get sick of it. But the public—that keeps you alive![2]

The habit of the heart called chutzpah is stock-in-trade among Manhattan taxi drivers. What makes this cabbie a paragon of citizenship is the way he combines chutzpah and humility. He welcomes strangers into his taxi, tells them what is on his mind, and listens to what they have to say. He uses the tensions of diversity and disagreement to open his mind to new possibilities: this is how he educates himself, and this is what makes him happy. If my taxi driver's enthusiasm for public life could be pumped into the nation's water supply, democracy's future would be assured.

Manhattan cabbies are well acquainted with the risks of public life, so they are not romantic about it: "You never know who's getting into the cab, so it's a little dangerous." Every cabbie passes up certain fares (as when one looks dangerously drunk) and avoids certain parts of the city at some hours (because other drivers have had trouble there). And yet even in the face of the risks, my driver was undaunted, perhaps because he knew that our ancient fear of the stranger is ironically and tragically misplaced. In America, "the majority of violent crimes are committed" not by strangers but "by people who know their victims."[3] Many of us project on the stranger the darkness within us or beside us that we do not want to acknowledge.

For my careening cabbie, the infrequent and oft-exaggerated dangers of public life were clearly outweighed by the benefits of interacting daily with strangers. He welcomed their company not merely because they helped him make his living—they helped him feel alive. As he practiced hospitality toward the stranger, he grew more at home, embracing rather than fearing the tensions of diversity as a path of learning and living.

A vital public life is key to democracy: the public realm is where we learn that despite our many differences, we really are in this together. It is where we have a chance to rub elbows with diversity and realize that "the other" not only lacks horns but may enrich and enliven us, that some kinds of tensions are educative, energizing, and even entertaining rather than threatening. Equally important, public life gives us a chance to size up what is happening in our world, speak our minds about it, hear others speak theirs, and perhaps join some of them in taking steps toward the kind of world we want.

Today, however, American public life is on the wane. More and more of us are becoming the kind of privatized person that Alexis de Tocqueville warned us about. Overly focused on family and friends, we are detached from—and sometimes actively afraid of—the strangers who are our fellow citizens. As Tocqueville pointed out, when our world is reduced to our kin and a few kindred spirits, we have lost our country.[4]

No Strangers Allowed

There is much we can do to revitalize our public life. But first we must understand the pivotal role public life plays in the dynamics of a free society and how and why it is eroding. That role becomes clear when we look at the three key layers of any society's structure: the private, the public, and the political. As we see how these three interact, we also see how the decline of our public life threatens the well-being of our political and private lives.

The ground floor of every society is the *private life*. Here we live our individual lives in conditions ranging from solitude to a handful of close relationships to expansive networks of friends and acquaintances. No matter what form they take, our private lives are always posted property: "NO STRANGERS ALLOWED EXCEPT BY INVITATION." Strangers have legitimate access to our private lives only when we say, "Come in"—perhaps because we need an electrician to fix a fuse box, perhaps because we want to make a new friend. When strangers walk into our private lives unbidden, we have a name for it: "crime." Private life is a sanctuary reserved for people we know and trust, not an arena where we meet the stranger as stranger.

Of all the levels on which we live, the private is the one we value most. Here our basic needs for food, shelter, and love are met, and we try to meet those needs in the people closest to us. America's founders made it clear how much they prized the private life when they established a nation that promised each citizen the right to "life, liberty and the pursuit of happiness." The founders believed that citizens who took advantage of that right to improve their own lot in life would turn around and use their gains to contribute to the common good.

Something happened on the way to the modern era. Many Americans seem to believe that this nation's entire reason for being is to secure such a self-contained private realm that we can pursue our own happiness without regard for the needs of others, even at their expense. Proof of that point is not hard to come by. It is difficult to gather Americans around issues of the common good, such as our shared responsibility to fund public education. We are quick to rally, however, when it looks like the government may "invade" our private lives by passing laws requiring the use of seat belts, banning us from owning assault weapons, or mandating the purchase of basic health insurance.

On the top level of any society are its structures of *political* power, a massive, interlocked collection of governmental and financial institutions that loom large over the private realm. The private life, by contrast, is a field of frail reeds, a congeries of isolated individuals who are vulnerable to central power. But there is nothing frail about the structures of power, not in a functional society.

Some Americans believe that a powerful central government is an unambiguous evil. Perhaps they have never been in a country where the government is so weak that private well-being is threatened by unchecked lawlessness and the absence of vital public services: *that* is a picture of evil. Nonetheless, it is true that a powerful central government—especially when it is neither transparent nor accountable—can deform the shape of our private lives in ways that isolated individuals are powerless to resist.

Many Americans have recently had vivid and painful reminders of that fact. Millions of us have lost jobs and homes because of high-level economic and political machinations that created great wealth for a few and devastation for the many. A significant number of these victims are, or were until recently, middle-class people who valued private life so much that they did not concern themselves with politics. America had always worked well for them, and they believed it would continue to do so.

Those of us who fall into that category are now getting a glimpse into the perennial plight of people for whom America has rarely, if ever, worked well. They have much to teach us. For Americans on the margin, who value private life as much as the rest of us, the private has never been an arena of security, sanctity, and strength to which they could retire. That is why most movements for social change have come from the ranks of the dispossessed. The poor—at least those whose capacity for action has not been gutted by debilitating poverty—have long understood that the power they need to pursue their *private* interests comes only as they band together as strangers with shared *public* interests to make their voices heard on high.

The political and the private differ in obvious respects. Still, they share a crucial characteristic: just as there are no strangers in our private lives, there are no strangers in the corridors of power. Congress and large corporations are akin to private clubs where memberships and access to the facilities cost big money. If you are an outsider who cannot afford the membership fee, your ability to get members of the club to listen to your needs is severely limited.

Yes, elected officials are held accountable by voters at the next election and are therefore sensitive to public opinion. And yes, corporations are often subject to consumer decisions and, in theory at least, to governmental oversight and regulation. But political power includes the ability to manipulate information and mitigate regulation in order to protect special interests against whatever threatens them.

Big money provides cover for political power, and political power provides cover for big money. The result is a closed system that can be held accountable only when "We the People" are sufficiently coherent to exercise countervailing power. And that, in turn, can happen only when we have access to a healthy public life in which we are willing to invest our time and energy.

The Meaning of Public Life

From anarchies to democracies to dictatorships, every kind of society has a private and political life of some sort. The distinguishing mark of a democratic society is a robust layer of *public* life—the natural habitat of "We the People"—which serves as a buffer zone between the private and the political. The presence of a public life does not guarantee democracy, but its absence guarantees that democracy cannot survive. Where there is no public life worthy of the name, the most likely political outcome is some form of authoritarian rule. And once authoritarian rule sets in, there can be no private life worthy of the name.

Public life is not easily defined. It embraces everything that is neither private nor political, which is a great deal indeed. However, we can get a start by tracking the word *public* itself, whose original meaning has largely been lost. We routinely use the word as a near synonym for *political,* conflating the two as if they were one. Candidates who stand for election are said to be running for "public office," meaning jobs in the political establishment. A "public school" refers to an educational institution mandated, guided, and funded by political processes. "Public policy" means legislation enacted by a political body.

But *public* is not synonymous with *political*. The word derives from the Latin *poplicus,* "pertaining to the people." Its distinct meaning begins to emerge when we learn that it is also related to the Latin *pubes* ("adult"), the same root from which we get the word *puberty.* The public life was originally understood as an arena for people who had moved beyond childhood into adulthood and were ready to take care of themselves and help take care of others. Weak and vulnerable prepubescent children who needed the protection provided by the private sphere were regarded as ready for neither the responsibilities nor the privileges of public life.[5]

It is worth noting that the word *private* comes from the Latin *privare,* the root that gives rise to the word *deprived.* How ironic that the private life so highly prized by Americans is a life that the ancients regarded as a form of deprivation for grown-ups. As my Manhattan cabbie said, "If you're with the same kind of people all the time, it's like wearing the same suit all the time—you get sick of it." What could be more stupefying for fully functional adults than to have nothing but a private life where one continually sees the same people and recycles the same experiences, attitudes, and ideas? No wonder the Greek word for a strictly private person was *idiotes,* from which we get the term *idiot,* meaning someone who says or does stupid things.

In modern usage, the word that most faithfully reflects the original meaning of *public* is *pub.* That word, of course, is shorthand for the English *public house,* an institution quite different from most American saloons, taverns, or bars. The typical English pub regularly hosts a cross section of the entire community. Everyone can be found there at one time or another, from babes in arms to middle-aged householders; from men and women heading home from work to those who are long retired; from neighbors who have known each other forever to strangers who are passing through. Amid this lively mix of characters, news and gossip are circulated, local issues are discussed, laughter and sometimes music fill the air, and the community weaves and reweaves itself day in and day out.

The pub is the kind of "great good place" that is vital to a democracy because it offers hospitality to all comers: it hosts a microcosm of the company of strangers.[6] In such places, we can continue to evolve beyond an ancient fear that threatens to undermine every creative form of human association, as noted by Abraham Lincoln in his 1859 campaign speech at the Wisconsin State Fair:

> From the first appearance of man upon the earth, down to very recent times, the words *stranger* and *enemy* were *quite,* or *almost,*

synonymous. Long after civilized nations had defined robbery and murder as high crimes, and had affixed severe punishments to them, when practiced among and upon their own people respectively, it was deemed no offence, but even meritorious, to rob, and murder, and enslave *strangers,* whether as nations or as individuals. Even yet, this has not totally disappeared.[7]

As long as we equate the stranger with the enemy, there can be no civil society, let alone a democracy where much depends on holding the tension of our differences without fearing or demonizing the other. It is no accident that Lincoln chose to discuss this vital topic (including a not-so-subtle allusion to slavery in America) at a state fair, another setting that, like the pub, offers hospitality to gatherings of strangers. As Lincoln went on to say on that occasion:

> Agricultural Fairs are becoming an institution of the country; they are useful in more ways than one; they bring us together, and thereby make us better acquainted, and better friends than we otherwise would be. . . . The man of the highest moral cultivation, in spite of all which abstract principle can do, likes him whom he *does* know, much better than him whom he does *not* know. To correct the evils, great and small, which spring from want of sympathy, and from positive enmity, among *strangers,* as nations, or as individuals, is one of the highest functions of civilization. To this end our Agricultural Fairs contribute in no small degree. They make more pleasant, and more strong, and more durable, the bond of social and political union among us.[8]

The Places and Purposes of Public Life

Public life happens in all the places and on all the occasions where strangers can freely mingle face-to-face, where our relations with each other have a chance to become "more pleasant, more strong, and more durable," thus enhancing "the bond of social and political union among us." The educators and activists Sara Evans and Harry Boyte call these "free spaces," by which they mean

> particular sorts of public places in the community [that] are the environments in which people are able to learn a new self-respect, a deeper and more assertive group identity, public skills, and values of cooperation and civic virtue. Put simply, free spaces are settings between private lives and large-scale institutions where ordinary citizens can act with dignity, independence, and vision.[9]

Here is a partial list of some of the settings where we have daily opportunities to experience the variety and vitality of the company of strangers. As you read through the list, think about the life-enhancing experiences you have had walking around your neighborhood, buying produce at a farmer's market, taking your kids to a playground or park, watching a Little League ball game, or enjoying a break in a coffee shop. Think, too, about how drab your life would be if places of this sort, where you can mingle with strangers, were not part of your experience:

- Residential neighborhoods
- Community gardens
- City streets and sidewalks
- Public transportation
- City parks and squares
- Cafés and coffee shops
- Galleries, museums, and libraries
- Street parties, carnivals, festivals, farmer's markets, art fairs, and flea markets
- Amateur and professional theatrical and sporting events
- Rallies, forums, hearings, and debates
- Voluntary associations, including "religious organizations, clubs, self-help and mutual aid societies, reform groups, neighborhood, civic, and ethnic groups"[10]

- Public schools, colleges, and universities
- Workplaces of many sorts
- Digital social media*

Settings such as these are so commonplace that we rarely think of the purposes they serve beyond the obvious. A street is a place for getting from one location to another; a café is a place to buy something to eat; a carnival is a place to have fun. But as Lincoln said of agricultural fairs, these venues of public life "are useful in more ways than one; they bring us together, and thereby make us better acquainted, and better friends than we otherwise would be."

The most vital purpose served by all such places is hidden in plain sight. They give us an experience of civic community beyond the narrow confines of private and political life. They offer us opportunities for creative interactions without which the social fabric of democracy soon becomes tattered and frayed and will unravel sooner or later. They allow strangers with intertwined fates a chance to keep restoring the fabric of a good society.

Look at what happens, day in and day out, in these vital public settings:

- Strangers meet on common ground.
- Fear of the stranger is reduced.
- Life is given color, texture, flair, drama, humor.
- People are drawn out of themselves.
- Common concerns are identified.
- Differences are debated.
- Conflict can be negotiated.
- Needs become evident, and mutual aid becomes possible.
- Ideas and resources can be shared and generated.
- People are empowered and protected against power.

---

*Because there are major differences between physical space and cyberspace in terms of their potentials and problems as gathering places for the company of strangers, I address online venues separately in Chapter VII.

In the company of strangers, we can learn that we are all in this together despite our many differences; that some of our differences are enriching and those that are vexing are negotiable; that it is possible to do business amicably with one another even in the face of conflicting interests. In the company of strangers, we can speak our minds aloud and listen as others speak theirs; in dialogue we may discover a common good in the midst of our diversity; and we have a chance to raise our voices to a level of audibility that none of us could achieve alone. When a society is rich in settings that offer opportunities of this sort, "We the People" can become a vital reality rather than a philosophical abstraction.

The ways in which a public life creates outcomes such as these range from subliminal to "in your face." Take, for example, what happens on that most elemental of public places, a city street. The simple act of walking down a crowded city sidewalk conveys a preconscious message that is key to democracy: it is possible for a large number of people, each of whom has a different goal, to get where they want to go without slamming into each other or shoving each other aside, planting the seeds of violence as they go. We simply need to learn the dance of public life—speeding up and slowing down, veering left and then right, until we have arrived at our destination safely and more or less on time.

On a crowded sidewalk, we develop bodily knowledge of how to negotiate our near collisions with a watchful grace that serves both our private interests and the common good. Contrast this with the bodily lesson learned by walking down an empty suburban or "edge city" sidewalk: you can go anywhere you want, by any route you want, at any speed you want, without having to consider the needs of others.

As I watch some of our elected leaders slam into each other and shove each other aside, escalating the verbal violence that helps makes our political life toxic, I wonder if walking to work every day might make them better leaders. As I watch some ordinary Americans behave in a similar style—often the most privileged Americans who need not mingle with the hoi polloi—I wonder if some long walks in the city might make better citizens of them.

Here is another example of what we can learn subliminally on the city streets. Years ago, as an organizer trying to help a suburban community embrace its growing diversity, I discovered that the people who are most afraid of strangers are those who have the least daily experience with them. Lock yourself up at home, take in enough fictional or sensationalized violence on television or online, and you are likely to be convinced that many strangers pose an immediate danger to your health. And yet if you negotiate crowds regularly in the course of your daily rounds, you learn that life on the streets is almost always safe and revitalizing. Not only are mayhem and murder extremely rare, but public experience can rescue us from the tedium of private life, energizing and sometimes entertaining us, all free of charge. We are more likely to feel comfortable about becoming engaged citizens if we experience these simple realities in the course of everyday life.

The streets also support democracy in ways that are not subliminal but strategic: witness the civil rights movement of the 1960s. African Americans, eventually accompanied by whites, took to the streets in growing numbers to protest racial injustice. The crowds that filled our thoroughfares, demanding their democratic rights with peaceful demonstrations, drew a level of popular attention that would never have been achieved with books, speeches, or letters to the editor, no matter how eloquent. When these nonviolent demonstrators were attacked by violent whites—some of them officers of the law armed with truncheons and trained attack dogs—popular opinion began to shift in favor of their cause. As a result, Congress was finally able to pass the 1965 Voting Rights Act (removing the remnants of Jim Crow that the 1964 Civil Rights Act had left untouched), 189 shameful years after we declared that "all men are created equal."

Study a list of settings that host the public life, and it soon becomes clear that each one offers a different kind of support for the company of strangers. In cafés and coffee shops, we can pause for a while in each other's presence, slowing the pace of our lives, overhearing conversations that might prove amusing, and perhaps exchanging a few words with someone we do not know. In bookstores and museums, we are in the presence of strangers who share our interests in certain topics or activities, providing a quiet sense of camaraderie. At rallies, forums, and debates, we can hear issues explored and speak our voices on them, practicing the accommodating dance of public life in verbal, not physical, space. In voluntary associations, we become better acquainted with each other and with the power of banding together to pursue shared goals.

In all of these everyday venues, we settle into the fact that we are part of a large, diverse, and sometimes problematic but often fascinating motley crew. If we use our opportunities in these settings wisely and well, we develop habits of the heart that not only make us better citizens but help us feel more at home on the face of the earth.

Public Power in a Democracy

To understand the importance of public life, imagine a society that lacks this critical intervening layer between private and political life. As it turns out, that does not take much imagination. The world is filled with societies of that sort—authoritarian, totalitarian, autocratic, despotic, and fascist societies—where centralized power reigns unchecked, free to invade private life in order to advance and protect its interests. In such societies, people protest abuses of power only at great personal risk. They, their families, and their friends may be punished in ways that range from becoming unemployable outcasts to being imprisoned and tortured to joining the ranks of "the disappeared."

The lesson of any authoritarian society is simple. Without a vital public to hold power accountable and protect individuals against its incursions, there can be neither a democratic polity nor a secure private life. Public life gives isolated individuals forums in which to join and amplify their voices, making it more likely that they will be heard by those in power. It also provides a communal shield to protect individuals against political manipulation and retribution, thus helping preserve the sanctity of private life.

It is easy to demonstrate the vital role public life plays in a democracy: when a society starts down the road to authoritarian rule, the first venues to be shut down are those that host the public life. People cannot gather on street corners without risking arrest. Public demonstrations are declared illegal and terminated with force. Voluntary associations, including religious communities, are forbidden, and all associational life must be approved by the powers that be. Faux political rallies are staged, scripted and choreographed by the regime. Fear—a primary tool of political control—is so deeply laced through the society that people no longer trust each other: isolated by law, force, and mutual distrust, individuals become pawns of central power and easy targets for neutralization or elimination.

The fear that autocrats generate and manipulate as a tool of social control mirrors their own fear of a vital public life. Unlike the political and the private, which are realms of relative order, the public is an arena of unpredictable and uncontrollable disorder. Things get noisy and messy when strangers gather, creating a yeasty mix of demographic differences and diverse interests, a tension-ridden and constantly shifting jumble of influences and alliances. Without this public vitality there would be no social ferment except, perhaps, underground. The public is the primordial soup that breeds new social life, the leaven that keeps our lives rising—and that potential for uprising is precisely what autocrats fear.

I am not a conspiracy theorist. I do not believe that there is a clandestine plot to seize power by weakening our public life (though the very public "plot" of America's oligarchy of wealth to commandeer our political process weakens every aspect of American democracy). And yet it is an observable fact that the critical public layer of democracy's infrastructure is eroding at a pace that barely attracts our attention and raises very few alarms: we are so obsessed with our private lives that we are largely oblivious to our public diminishments. If we continue to ignore the decline of our public life—the decline of vital energies that help animate democracy—the private life we cherish will ultimately be undermined.

A major sign of this decline is the fact that the commercial function of many public streets has been replaced by privately owned shopping malls. From ancient Greece until the mid-twentieth century, commerce on the public streets was the primary magnet that drew strangers together in ways that helped create a public. Yes, strangers still gather in the malls. But malls put limits on who can gather and what they can do, limits that undermine some of the key contributions that public life makes to a democracy. Beggars and the homeless are banned from shopping malls, pushing these marginalized people even further off the radar of civic empathy. Explicit political activity is banned as well, largely with the support of the courts.[11] When was the last time you heard a soapbox orator or witnessed a political demonstration in one of our cathedrals of consumerism, even in the parking lot? If you have seen a beggar or a rally in a mall, odds are that what you saw lasted a very short while before private security guards arrived to "clean things up."

There is a reason for all this, of course. The owners of the private property called malls have one overriding interest: to create an environment conducive to shopping. To that end, they may support noncontroversial community activities, such as Salvation Army solicitations, Suzuki concerts by local schoolchildren, indoor arts and crafts exhibits, a farmer's market in the parking lot. They will not, however, allow their property to be used to debate political issues or remind us of certain unpleasant social realities lest people experience stress and tension that would diminish the "joy of shopping."

The Decline of Public Life

As malls replace city streets as our primary places of commerce and the seductions of consumerism trump the imperatives of citizenship, we are deprived of the primary setting where strangers have interacted freely throughout history. Are we so wedded to shopping that we will give up the ferment of public life, and some of our key rights as citizens, in favor of a private commercial venue free of the civic dynamics that help secure a democracy?

A simple mental experiment will demonstrate what we have lost as malls have replaced America's public streets: try to imagine the civil rights movement of the 1960s happening today. As you do, remember that what happened back then—unlike the widely publicized "tea party" rallies of 2009 and 2010—was a movement of "invisible" people who had no standing in our society, no secret financial backers with deep pockets, and no cable networks or political infotainment "personalities" to serve as their megaphones.[12]

What power does a street demonstration have when no one is on the streets to see it? When it does not interfere with shopping in order to snap us out of our consumer trance into some form of citizen response? When the media give it no attention? A twenty-first-century civil rights movement would be hard-pressed to find a stage as compelling as city streets.

Online social media are often touted as a contemporary form of public space. Clearly, they have their potential, which I explore in Chapter VII, but they have limits too. When we interact face-to-face, our sense of belonging to a civic community is literally embodied in ways that cannot be replicated by words and images on digital displays. When we come together in the flesh for reasons ranging from commerce to celebration, we absorb inarticulate and irreplaceable bone-deep knowledge of what it means to be the "body politic."

The rise of privately owned malls, with the legal limitations they impose on the formation of civic community, is only one example of how our public life is becoming impoverished. In nearly every traditional setting of public life, our daily opportunities for face-to-face encounters with strangers are contracting, not expanding:

- How many of us get to work each day via public transportation where we spend time among people we do not know? Many of us drive to work solo, park in a lot or garage, take an elevator or make a short walk to the office, encountering very few strangers en route.

- How many of us attend political rallies or debates, rubbing elbows with people of diverse viewpoints onsite, applauding when we agree with what is said and letting the speaker know when we do not?

Most of us sit in our living rooms watching such events on TV, jumping to the latest hot sitcom or "reality" show when "all that political stuff" begins to bore us.

• How many of us have the leisure to enjoy public parks, visit a museum, shop at a local farmer's market, or attend a festival or fair? Many things—including the economic pressures that compel people to work long hours, sometimes at more than one job—have robbed us of leisure time, and many communities can no longer give much support to the kinds of settings where we once spent such time.

• How many of us have gone to a public library or a bookstore lately to look for good reading material? Many of us now receive our reading material electronically and order books online for home delivery. Public libraries across the country have had to cut staff, services, and hours due to lack of funding, and many independent bookstores have gone out of business along with many branches of the major chains.

• How many of us have gone to a movie theater lately to see the latest cinema sensation amid a crowd of strangers? The majority of Americans now watch movies in private "home entertainment centers." As a result, many smaller communities no longer have the downtown theater that was once a major public space.

• How many of us are fully present to strangers even when we are surrounded by them? When we walk the streets, ride the bus, or sit in coffee shops and cafés, many of us are electronically connected to places other than where we are and people other than those we are with.

• How many of us are actively involved in voluntary associations that represent a wide range of human differences? Many such organizations are composed of people with similar life experiences and beliefs, making them extensions of private life instead of microcosms of public life.

• How many of us know much about the people who live in our neighborhood or show up daily in our workplace? Many of us interact so infrequently with colleagues or neighbors that we fail to forge the kind of relationships that would strengthen the body politic.

The answers to these questions do not point to the Apocalypse. They do suggest, however, that we are an increasingly private and therefore deprived people, deprived of meaningful opportunities to develop democratic habits of the heart. They also suggest that we must reclaim our public life before we sink any further into privatism at the expense of democracy *and* of the privacy we cherish, a privacy that requires public vigilance if it is to be preserved.

I believe it is possible to do just that in every venue of our lives, including the ubiquitous shopping mall. Despite the democratic downside of malls, they are the places where many people are most likely to find themselves among strangers on a regular basis. What can we do to redeem the malls in service of democracy?

The possibilities may be limited. Still, they open up a bit when we stop looking at malls as monolithic private preserves and focus instead on the privately owned businesses that rent space in them, as their predecessors rented space on the city streets. Of course, these rental agreements include rules regarding what tenants may and may not do, and many mall businesses are not local stores but franchises licensed by large corporations that have their own rules. The owner-operator of a mall-based McDonald's has less freedom about what can happen on site than the owner of a Main Street burger shop.

But suppose a few local owners became convinced that certain kinds of nonpartisan, prepolitical activity are good for business—which they are—and began hosting such activities in their own stores? There are precedents for this. Bookstores, from local independents to small chains, often host author readings that bring strangers together in conversation, sometimes around political topics, building community and business simultaneously.

There is no reason why such conversations need to be limited to bookstores. Here is a notice for an August 21, 2008, evening gathering at Schneider Drugstore in Minneapolis:

> Millions of Americans have been activated by political campaigns
> this year. But what comes after the elections? How can we build

on this energy to create civic change? Harry Boyte, author of *The Citizen Solution: How You Can Make a Difference,* will lead an open discussion. . . . Tom Sengupta, the owner of Schneider Drugstore, hosts "Tom's Drugstore," a monthly meeting where people of different ages, views and backgrounds mix it up on different political and public affairs topics. Each discussion begins with two or three short reflections, and then people jump in. Tom's Drugstore follows in the tradition of the Humphrey drugstore in Doland, South Dakota. In Doland, Hubert Humphrey's father's drugstore was the civic center of town.[13]

In the midst of our increasingly privatized lives, we can still "go public" if we choose to do so. Returning briefly to some of the problems I touched on earlier, here are some possibilities:

• We could drive to work with more than one person to a car, a common practice during times when gas is either rationed or prohibitively priced.

• We could get out of the house more often for something other than going to work or the mall. We could attend political rallies, buy food at the local farmer's market, visit the public library, go to a concert. Once we start experimenting with public options for meeting certain needs and pursuing certain interests, we might learn that they have life-giving features that trump their "inconvenience."

• When we are in public places such as the mall or a coffee shop, we can be there unplugged and unwired. We might find that sometimes the public life is as entertaining, even as musical, as what comes to us through ear buds.

• We could meet people outside our small circle of family and friends by volunteering for visitations an hour or two a week at a nearby hospital, joining a voluntary association, or simply taking time to ask neighbors or colleagues how they are. As we do so, we might discover that we are revitalizing our own lives as well as helping revitalize the public life.

Reclaiming Space for Public Life

Ask Americans what must be done to repair American politics, and most responses will focus on "them," the people who hold elective office and the governing bodies in which they serve. It is an understandable mistake: our headline news is dominated by people and events at the centers of political power. But it *is* a mistake. The most important thing "We the People" can do to restore democracy is to restore the venues and vitality of the public life that we have opportunities to participate in on a daily basis. Only via local connections, multiplied many times over, can citizens hope to generate the level of people power necessary to effect political change.

One key to renewing our public life is to reclaim the hospitable physical space it requires. The great names associated with urban design—Jane Jacobs, William H. Whyte, James Rouse, and the landscape architect Frederick Law Olmstead—all gave high priority to creating settings that support the interaction of strangers. For example, as they reconfigured an old city or planned a new one, they favored multiple-use spaces, knowing that they will generate more interest, safety, and enjoyment—and therefore a greater variety and volume of public life—than single-purpose spaces can.

The theory is simple. You will find a lively public life if, within the boundaries of an urban neighborhood, you find housing and shopping, a park and a public school, workplaces and places of worship, a movie theater, a coffee shop, and a bar. That kind of neighborhood will be in use much of the day and night by people of many descriptions: homeowners maintaining their property, employees going to and from work, children going to and from school, parents and children playing in the park, shoppers and shopkeepers doing business, people seeking entertainment or chances to socialize. The presence of this mixed company not only makes an urban neighborhood more interesting and appealing but also enhances public safety. A space with nothing except offices that empty out in the late afternoon, leaving the streets deserted after dark, is dangerous for the hapless nighttime pedestrian.

Few of us hold posts that give us direct influence on decisions about urban design. Still, all of us are citizens who have a right to be heard before the planning and zoning commissions responsible for those decisions—commissions that normally hear more from people concerned about profit than they do from people concerned about the quality of our public life. We need to make the case that profit and public life are not incompatible but symbiotic: a healthy public life enhances private economic values even as it enhances the political values of a democracy.

In some locales, citizens have found ways to reclaim public space more directly than testifying before a commission. In Portland, Oregon, the urban designer Mark Lakeman was struck by the absence of the village plaza or piazza, a traditional public space that has been sacrificed to the needs of the automobile. Our "crossroads"—that conjunction of well-traveled routes where strangers once encountered each other and exchanged news and views—has become a mere intersection where vehicles turn the corner and pedestrians cross the street. In a process of erosion so slow that we accept it as the norm, the efficient movement of traffic now dominates the space where people traditionally met and mingled and strengthened their communal bonds.

So Lakeman and his neighbors did two things.[14] First, they "formed the City Repair Project, a volunteer-run nonprofit that set out to change the way Portlanders think about the places where people come together."[15] Second, they went to work redesigning a key intersection in their neighborhood without seeking official permission. Their purpose was simple: to take a place where nobody lingered and make it one where people wanted to hang out. Their approach was also simple, as Lakeman explains:

> At our first project, the neighbors who lived around the intersection came out on the weekend, painted a design in the street, built all these structures around the corners—a bench, a lending library, a 24-hour tea stand, a children's playhouse, a kiosk for sharing neighborhood information—and turned it into an interactive

social space. . . . That was years ago. . . . Since then people have . . . put in gardens, helped each other paint their houses. Americans move every four to seven years, and that period of time is visibly lengthening right around that intersection because people want to live there. Families are clustering around it . . . so there are more children—and more shared childcare, and more adults interacting with kids on the street.[16]

What were the repercussions of the fact that these citizen activists did not ask official permission to reclaim public space? Not the "cease and desist" order that you might expect. The value of what they had done soon became so evident that "the city passed an ordinance allowing neighborhoods to build gathering places in street intersections."[17] And that, says Lakeman, freed up all kinds of energies for neighborhood renewal:

> After everything you see on TV or in politics, you would think that asking a group of Americans to sit down and work out something like this would be difficult. But it's not. People sit down for a potluck, and maybe that very evening they start talking about what they want to do. This year, we're going to reach a total of over 200 major sites and almost 300 little projects that have been built.[18]

"Build it and they will come!" may be a cliché, but it works, especially if *they* help build it. Lakeman's group created "strange attractors" in easily accessible places that drew people out of their houses and into each other's lives. Their involvement with one another was not so deep as to become burdensome, but it was deep enough to let them experience the reassuring fact that they live among people who are aware of and care about each other.

The idea of strange attractors helps us understand the renewal of public life as a human-scale enterprise in which ordinary citizens can participate. I live in a town where many people jog. On one of the joggers' favorite streets, a homeowner took a garden hose, a short length of pipe, and a spigot and created a free water stand for thirsty runners, complete with paper cups. The homeowner is retired—from coaching track, among other things—so he has time to sit on his front lawn and kibitz with those who stop for a drink. *Voilà!* The public life!

When James Rouse created the "new town" of Columbia, Maryland, instead of attaching a mailbox to the front of each house, he clustered them in a centrally located kiosk where people would go to get their mail and meet each other in the process. *Voilà!* The public life!

Strange attractors are simple, they work, and the reason they work is clear: deep in all of us is the instinct that being connected to one another is happier, healthier, and safer than living in isolation.

The Promise of Neighborhoods

For many of us, the strangers closest at hand are our neighbors. There was a time when that statement would have made no sense, when people who lived side by side knew each other at least slightly. Neighborliness has declined for reasons ranging from the disappearance of the front porch to the rise of the two-wage-earner family to online networks and e-mail replacing face-to-face conversation. And yet people still live side by side. Despite the obstacles to neighborliness, some have acted creatively to strengthen neighborhood bonds, aiding and abetting democracy in the process.[19]

Creativity of this sort often kicks in when there is an urgent problem to be solved. Take, for example, the neighborhood watch programs that have helped stem crime in urban and rural communities alike, programs that are the equivalent of putting the front porch back on people's homes.[20] Now, instead of locking the doors and pulling the shades, neighbors take turns "standing watch" around the clock, keeping an eye on what is happening in their community.[21] When they see suspicious activity, they call the police, turn on lights, and make noise, sending a clear message that this neighborhood is not easy picking for criminals.

These programs have proved to be safer and more effective than private solutions like handguns, which are often involved in murderous arguments between family members or friends or in tragic accidents involving children playing "cops and robbers."[22] The safest communities are not those with private arsenals, which can make private life more dangerous. They are those with a public life in which citizens take care of each other as well as themselves.[23]

But why wait for crime to inspire us to strengthen our neighborhoods? A neighborhood association, or a handful of enterprising neighbors, can do many simple things to encourage people to come out of isolation for a while and enjoy each other's company, developing a stronger sense of civic community in the process.[24] In one neighborhood where I lived, a few families organized an outdoor potluck supper every summer. The street was closed off for a block, tables were set up on the pavement, people brought food and lawn chairs, some brought musical instruments, and many hung out until the sun went down or the kids needed to go to bed. The investment of time and energy was small. The returns on neighborliness were substantial.

In that same neighborhood, local schoolteachers enlisted the help of neighbors to create a community garden, giving residents a place to socialize as they grew vegetables and the teachers an outdoor classroom for their elementary school students.[25] And a neighborhood association sponsored several annual holiday gatherings that allowed nearby neighbors to meet and make friends among what would otherwise have been a relatively faceless collection of commuters.

In yet another neighborhood, under the auspices of a community foundation, people deepened their social bonds through a "neighborhood resource catalog." Neighbors were invited to submit descriptions of services they would be willing to volunteer, which were then distributed in print (and today could be posted on a Web site). The catalog contained a wide range of offerings: some people were willing to take care of a pet while a family was on vacation; others volunteered to visit shut-ins; still others offered to share their skill by making minor home repairs.

To keep anyone from being locked in to a promise that turned out not to be working well, services were time-limited (say, to three hours of home repair services per week), and all entries had a life span of three months, at which point they could be renewed or allowed to expire. The catalog urged people to use common sense to avoid any sort of exploitation, and the coalition of local congregations that screened, published, and monitored entries provided an additional safety net. This kind of project clearly requires more time, effort, and organizational support than a potluck supper, but the social benefits are proportionally greater.

This same community foundation sponsored another project called "Living Room Seminars on Coping with Community Change." The project was aimed at a cluster of neighborhoods where rapid demographic changes were creating the kind of anxiety that can lead to unscrupulous real estate practices and community deterioration. The seminars were based on a six-session curriculum led by trained discussion leaders who gathered with small groups of neighbors in someone's living room to explore their fears and hopes about the future of the community. Like any respectable seminar, these were fueled by coffee and cookies as well as good ideas.

As this project spread, it helped stabilize the community in several ways. It gave residents a chance to look at their fears in the light of day, where they seemed less ominous. It invited people to recall prior experiences of change in their lives, to realize that many of them had had positive outcomes and to remember whatever it was that had helped see them through. It allowed longtime residents to meet some of the newcomers, putting a human face on social change and providing the reassurance that comes from confronting challenges and envisioning opportunities together.

Several of the projects mentioned here were initiated, organized, or backed by a neighborhood association or a community foundation. While there is much that individuals can do to renew our public life, some sort of established civic organization is obviously helpful in creating and maintaining channels for individual involvement. Seattle provides a notable case study in its creation of a "department of neighborhoods." Its mission is

> to bring government closer to the residents of Seattle by engaging them in civic participation; by helping them become empowered to

make positive contributions to their communities; and by involving more of Seattle's underrepresented residents, including communities of color and immigrants, in civic discourse, processes, and opportunities.[26]

For the past twenty years, Seattle has been dotted with semi-autonomous neighborhood councils led by elected officials whose functions include enacting policy and allocating public money:[27]

> Begun . . . in response to citizen concerns over crime, drugs and growth management, the program was designed to provide residents a greater say in the allocation of tax dollars. [Since its inception], residents have leveraged city matching funds with their own resources and labor to create more than 3,000 community projects, including new playgrounds and art installations. An unintended consequence of the neighborhood councils seems to be an informed, engaged public that routinely scores higher on measure of civic health than is the case in comparable cities. "We've been able to build a much stronger sense of community here," says Jim Diers, author . . . and founding director of the city's Department of Neighborhoods. "And in the process, our attitude toward city hall has changed, our sense of government has changed. It's not just something that spends our tax dollars; it's something that's an extension of who we are as citizens."[28]

This story underscores the vital role that government can play in the renewal of public life when it creates public policy to help drive citizen engagement instead of waiting for citizen engagement to help drive public policy.[29] As the sociologist Carmen Sirianni has said, "Government invests in a lot of things. Why not civic engagement?"[30] Why not, indeed, if our democracy is truly one of "We the People"?

Imagining the Public Life

I have emphasized the importance of face-to-face experience of the stranger as we form and nurture democratic habits of the heart. While experience can change the way we look at the world, the converse is also true: the way we look at the world can change the meaning of our experience.

For example, I am walking down the street when a homeless man approaches and asks me for money. Setting aside the question of whether I should give him what he asks for, the quality of this encounter with "otherness" depends on the kind of imagination I bring to it, which shapes how I approach it, how I engage it, and what I take from it.

Through the lens of a fearful imagination, I see this man as a threat. He is disheveled, he smells bad, and I assume that he is physically or mentally ill. By asking me for money, he is doing something not done in polite society *and* pricking my conscience about the vast contrast between my affluence and his poverty. Even more challenging, he has forced me to look directly into the eyes of poverty and homelessness, a reality I would prefer to ignore; now I have to suppress the fact that I have seen a human being clinging to the edge of the cliff. So I internalize the experience with feelings of annoyance or anger about the way this stranger has penetrated my zone of studied ignorance and disturbed my mind.

Alternatively, I might interpret this experience through the lens of what C. Wright Mills called the "sociological imagination."[31] Now the homeless beggar serves as a data point through which I can see the flawed pattern of American society. He reminds me that the richest nation on earth does not have a safety net to catch people as they free-fall to the bottom of the pit and that something like one-quarter of the adult homeless in America are veterans.[32] I walk away from him thinking like a social engineer about possibilities ranging from relief programs to strategies for income redistribution.

Or I might interpret this experience through the lens of compassionate imagination. The literal translation of *compassion* is "feeling *with*"—and a big story is hidden in that little word *with*. According to the dictionary, the word is "used to indicate that somebody is ... in the *company* of another person," and the root meaning of *company* is "person *with* whom one is breaking bread." When I see the homeless beggar through compassionate eyes, I am able to say, "This man and I sit at the same table and eat food from the same source. Our lives and fates are intertwined, and I must act accordingly."

How precisely *you* must act is not mine to dictate. That is your ethical decision to make. My point is simply this: if our experience in the company of strangers is to deepen our sense of civic community and help us cultivate democratic habits of the heart, the lens of compassionate imagination is crucial.

Wendell Berry is a writer whose compassionate imagination is unsurpassed. He is the author of a series of novels about a Kentucky town called Port William, with a cast of characters that stretches across three generations. Port William is a small farming community whose residents are not strangers to each other in the way city people are. Still, they remain strangers to each other in the way *all* of us are, no matter how well we may think we know each other: within each of us there is an endless, inarticulate play of shadow and light that makes us riddles to each other because we are riddles to ourselves.

And yet all of the characters in this fictional world are integral and valued parts of what Berry calls "the Port William membership." With this phrase he names a fabric of belonging that is vital to sustaining the diverse and sundry lives of Port William's citizens, whatever their strengths and weaknesses may be. Take, for example, the woman whose story is told in Berry's novel *Hannah Coulter:*

> The story encompasses Hannah's life, including the Great Depression, World War II, the postwar industrialization of agriculture, the flight of youth to urban employment, and the consequent remoteness of grandchildren. The tale is told in the voice of an old woman twice widowed, who has experienced much loss yet has never been defeated. Somehow, lying at the center of her strength is the "membership"—the fact that people care for each other and, even in absence, hold each other in a kind of presence.[33]

This sense of membership is the ultimate gift of the public life. As Berry points out in an essay on some of the themes that run through his novels, our sense that we belong to one another and therefore cannot be "as self-centered as [we] please" comes not from "egalitarianism and tolerance" but from "knowledge, an understanding of the necessity of . . . differences, and respect. Respect, I think, always implies imagination—the ability to see one another, across our inevitable differences, as living souls."[34]

If we aim to be "one nation, indivisible," the capacity to imagine ourselves as members of one another, despite all that separates us, is essential. As Berry says, "If what we see and experience . . . does not become real in imagination, then it never can become real to us, and we are forever divided from it."[35] That is why I now turn to classrooms and congregations, settings in which many of us develop the lenses of imagination through which we receive and interpret our world.

[CHAPTER VI]

Classrooms and Congregations

Did you, too, O friend, suppose democracy was only for elections, for politics, and for a party name? I say democracy is only of use there that it may pass on and come to its flower and fruit in manners, in the highest forms of interaction between [people], and their beliefs—in religion, literature, colleges and schools—democracy in all public and private life.

—WALT WHITMAN, "Democratic Vistas"[1]

In 1974, as I was plotting out a sabbatical, I visited several communities where my family and I might spend the following year. With three young children to think about, checking out the local elementary school was always part of my itinerary. At one of those schools, as I walked into a classroom, my eyes were drawn to the very large American flag hanging from a flagpole. Then I saw what was hung on a hook next to the flag—a wooden paddle heavy enough to do serious damage to a child's body and spirit.

I asked the principal what the paddle was for. I knew the answer, of course, but I was hoping he would tell me that they were collecting artifacts for a museum of old-time public school horrors. "Oh," he said casually, "that's how we deal with kids who get out of line. Sometimes just the sight of the paddle is enough to do the trick. Even so, we need to use it every now and then."

That, of course, is a story about the power of schools to form or deform our habits of the heart. There was the American flag, a symbol of "life, liberty and the pursuit of happiness" and a reminder of all that it takes to maintain a democracy. And there was the wooden paddle, used to exercise social control in the same way a totalitarian society uses the police and the military: put them on display hoping that will do the trick, and be ready to shoot if necessary.

The K–12 classrooms where we all spend much of our youth—and the college and university classrooms where about one-quarter of us earn postsecondary degrees—are the venues in which we are most likely to be formed or deformed as citizens. Most schools do not do this job as poorly as the one I visited in 1974, and some of them do it very well. Today, however, high-stakes testing has deflected many of our public schools from their historical function of forming good citizens, and higher education is more focused on training employees than on instilling democratic habits of the heart.

After classrooms, the congregations where adherents of most faith traditions gather on a regular basis are the settings in which our habits of the heart are most likely to be formed or deformed. It is hard to know the true frequency with which Americans attend religious services because claiming a religious affiliation is more popular than actually having one. But according to the best estimates, roughly one-third of us can be found at some form of worship at least once or twice a month.[2] So except for classrooms and the workplace, Americans probably spend more hours in congregational settings than in any other setting where there is collective intentionality and formal leadership.

Alexis de Tocqueville understood that what happens in classrooms and congregations would be crucial to the future of American democracy. He had especially high hopes for public schools, which as early as the 1830s were places where Americans were developing democratic habits of the heart. As the biographer Leo Damrosch writes, Tocqueville was struck by the fact that "elementary education was available to an ever-growing segment of the population, enabling a sophisticated political consciousness that was still unimaginable in France."[3]

Tocqueville's take on the role of religious communities was more ambivalent. He had abandoned much of the Roman Catholic belief system in which he had grown up, but his liturgical formation was deep: convinced that Catholic formality was the norm for Christian worship, he looked askance at the spontaneous, emotionally charged, and unpredictable expressions of evangelical Christianity common in the America of his time.[4] As Damrosch comments:

> In this area . . . Tocqueville's objectivity failed him. Not only did he exaggerate the irrationality of evangelical religion, but he missed its social role in addressing the anxieties of the American people that would be central to his own analysis.[5]

Fortunately, Tocqueville had a positive experience with another religious group whose mode of worship was quite different from both evangelicals and Catholics: the Quakers of Philadelphia. The Religious Society of Friends, as Quakers are formally known, "had long encouraged cooperation in public affairs as well as toleration in religion" and were actively involved in various forms of relief work and associational life.[6] Tocqueville's appreciation of Quakerism—perhaps because the gravitas of the Quaker silent meeting for worship met his standards of religious formality—gave him his first insight into what would become a major theme of his work: the importance of voluntary associations in forming democratic habits of the heart.

Tocqueville is one of many who have wondered whether religious communities can serve American democracy well. It is true that religious convictions have sometimes divided us. But divisiveness is far from the whole story of religion's role in human history.[7] In light of the fact that religious communities have been our most prominent form of voluntary associational life from the Plymouth Colony to the present, congregations must rank high on any list of settings where Americans develop their habits of the heart.

Classrooms and congregations have the potential to make major contributions to the cause of democracy. However, there are obstacles to consider before teachers, clerics, and lay leaders who feel led to do so can take up that cause. I want to examine some of these obstacles and explore how we might surmount them in hopes of advancing democracy's agenda in these settings where we spend so many hours of our lives.

Where Classrooms and Congregations Converge

I honor the American principle that state functions such as public education must neither encourage nor impede personal decisions about religious belief. So for much of this chapter, I will treat classrooms and congregations separately. But before I take education and religion down two different tracks, I want to look at one important way in which they converge: in both settings, there is power to form us inwardly in ways that can undermine or enhance our capacity to play a creative role in a democratic society.

The philosopher Jacob Needleman has written that "one of the great purposes of the American nation is to shelter and guard the rights of all men and women to seek the conditions and the companions necessary for the inner search."[8] He refers, of course, to the First Amendment's prohibition of an established religion and the freedom of choice it assures us in our search for purpose and meaning. But we make a mistake if we think that religious institutions have a lock on influencing our "inner search." Educational institutions have at least as much impact, and arguably more, on our basic assumptions about what is real, possible, and meaningful.

Whether the subject is the human or the nonhuman world, we get much more than facts in the classroom. Consciously and unconsciously, we get images of ourselves (for example, as contestants in a win-lose competition or persons of unconditional worth) and images of the world (for instance, as "a war of all against all" or an interdependent community) that help form our inner lives. That is why it is lamentable, even tragic, that public education's chance to play a positive role in the inner search that lies at the heart of being human has been crimped by an overly broad interpretation of the First Amendment's prohibition of state-sponsored religion.

For fear of violating the rightful separation of church and state, we have imposed unnecessary limits on our schools when it comes to helping students deal with nondoctrinal inner issues—such as the nature of a "good life" and what it requires of us—that can make or break a democracy. Democracy loses when teachers feel they are skating on thin ice if they invite students to wrestle with questions such as those Rabbi Hillel famously asked: "If I am not for myself, who is for me? If I am only for myself, what am I? If not now, when?"[9] What questions could be more relevant to forming the habits of the heart that democracy requires, and by what standard do they violate the First Amendment?

I realize that *I* am skating on thin ice here, so I want to be transparent about my own convictions regarding the separation of church and state. I am a Quaker whose spiritual ancestors were persecuted, imprisoned, and occasionally executed for their beliefs by officials of the established church in England. When they arrived in America in search of religious liberty, they met with similar treatment at the hands of intolerant Puritans. On Boston Common you will find a statue in memory of Mary Dyer, a middle-aged Quaker mother of six who was hanged in 1660 before a crowd of churchgoers and civic leaders bent on safeguarding their "Godly" order against her seditious belief in the "inner light."

So I am no fan of the "good old days" of state-sponsored religion, or of the religious arrogance that says, "Our truth is the only truth." As I argue for public education's right—and obligation—to engage students with questions of meaning, I want neither to violate the separation of church and state nor to encourage people who would impose their religious beliefs on others.

However, I am equally passionate about not wanting to violate the deepest needs of the human soul, which our educational system does with some regularity. An education that pretends to explore only the outer world is disingenuous and incomplete. A good education is intentional and thoughtful about helping students find an inner orientation toward what is "out there" that will be life-giving for them and the world. In education as well as religion, we must find ways to help people conduct an inner search free of any predetermined outcome while providing them with the guidance and resources they need to conduct it well. As we do so, we will be shaping some of the habits of the heart that make democracy possible.

We can take a big step toward freeing teachers to help students with their "inner search" by shaking off the mistaken notion that this is code language for the search for God. Inner-life questions are the kind that our students (and their teachers and parents) ask regularly, with or without God talk: "Do I have gifts that the world wants and needs?" "Does my life have meaning and purpose?" "Whom and what can I trust?" "How can I rise above my fears?" "How do I deal with suffering, my own and that of my family and friends?" "How can I maintain hope?" "What does my life mean in the face of the fact that I am going to die?"

The poet Rainer Maria Rilke once engaged in an extended correspondence with a student named Franz Kappus. This nineteen-year-old pressed question after question on his literary idol and always received thoughtful answers, resulting in Rilke's famous book, *Letters to a Young Poet*. After addressing each of Kappus's urgent queries on its own terms, Rilke offers wise counsel for seekers of any age and for their teachers:

> Be patient toward all that is unresolved in your heart. . . . Try to love the questions themselves. . . . Do not now seek the answers, which cannot be given because you would not be able to live them—and the point is to live everything. *Live the questions now.* Perhaps you will then gradually, without noticing it, live along some distant day into the answers.[10]

Creating conditions under which students can conduct an inner search does not mean dictating answers to inner-life questions, which by definition do not have answers in any conventional sense. It means helping students learn how to ask questions that are worth asking because they are worth living, questions one can fruitfully hold at the center of one's life.

Public Education and the Inner Search

None of this means that we must add a course on the "inner search" to the curriculum, let alone one on religion. Inner-life questions are embedded in *all* the subjects we teach, *if* we teach them not merely as collections of facts and concepts but also as fields of meaning. The most obvious examples are literature and the arts, where questions of meaning are on the surface. Studying such classics as Robert Penn Warren's *All the King's Men* or *The Diary of Anne Frank* clearly gives teachers a chance to explore important issues related to democratic habits of the heart. But every subject, rightly understood, has the potential to shed light on the question at the heart of every religious and secular search for meaning and purpose: *How can I connect with something larger than my own ego?*

Why does a good historian care about the "dead" past? To show us that it is still alive because we are connected to it in ways we often do not understand. Why does a good biologist care about "mute" nature? To show us that nature "speaks" to us about the impact of our actions, calling us to honor our connection to the natural world. Why does a good literary scholar care about "fictional" worlds? To show us that our deepest connection with reality comes not merely from mastering facts but from engaging them with our imaginations.

No educational task is more important than helping students reflect on realities larger than their own egos—and learn how to find meaning and purpose by connecting with realities that bring life, not death. Our species has made many responses to the yearning for connectedness, with outcomes that have ranged from heavenly to hellish. The dream of human equality that gave meaning to the life of Martin Luther King Jr.

moved us closer to the liberation of oppressed and oppressor alike. The nightmare myth of Aryan superiority in "blood, soil, and race" that filled the emptiness of many German lives in the ruins of the Weimar Republic took millions of innocents into the depths of hell.

How can we teach conventional subjects in a way that allows students to reflect on critical choices such as these? The single most important thing teachers can do is explicitly connect the "big story" of the subject with the "little story" of the student's life.[11] Doing so helps us make progress toward two vital educational goals. We accelerate our students' learning of challenging subjects because they will put more energy into pursuing issues they see as related to their own lives. We support their search for meaning and purpose by giving them information, concepts, and critical tools around questions they care about.

A story from my own education illustrates the point. I was taught the history of the Holocaust at some of the best schools in the country. And yet because I was taught the big story with no attention to the little story—and was given no guidance on how to connect the Holocaust's horrors to the pleasant realities of my own life—I held what I learned as if all this evil had happened on some other planet to some other species. My teachers taught me in the same way they had been taught, delivering objective facts without attending to the student's subjective self. As a result, I was distanced from the murderous realities of the Third Reich, leaving me with less understanding of history *and* of myself than a good education should.

Only after I completed my schooling was I able to make two important connections between the big story of the Holocaust and the little story of my own life. First, the community in which I grew up practiced systematic discrimination against Jews. If you were a Jew on the North Shore of Chicago during the 1950s, you did not live in Wilmette or Kenilworth or Winnetka. You lived in a gilded ghetto called Glencoe created by the same anti-Semitism that gave rise to the massive evil of Hitler's Germany. That evil did not happen to another species on another planet. It happened to people I cared about in a place that I knew well. Knowing that would have helped me understand why—as a young person whose best friend happened to be Jewish—I felt vaguely ill at ease in my own community.

The second thing I failed to learn was closer to the bone and more ethically urgent. Within me is a power of darkness that may tempt me to want to "kill you off" when you threaten some concept of reality or morality that I cherish. I will not do it with a weapon but with a mental dismissal, some way of putting you into a category of people whose opinions mean nothing to me. Now I no longer need to be bothered by your otherness or by the tension it creates in me. That, it seems to me, is the spiritual equivalent of murder: I have rendered you utterly irrelevant to my life.

By failing to intersect the big story with the little story, my history teachers left me with facts about the horrors of the Holocaust that never came to life. They also left me with a life that went unchallenged by those horrors until many years later.[12] By keeping me outside of the subject—and keeping the subject outside of me—my teachers delivered a profoundly flawed education. I learned neither about the Holocaust as it really was nor about myself as I really am.

Of course, deep and penetrating self-knowledge often does not come until our later years. Still, the groundwork for it can and should be laid early, which involves no great effort. For example, I might have been shown demographic data about the North Shore and asked to advance a theory about why the population distribution was so skewed by religion or ethnicity. I might have been asked to interview adults whose lives had been touched by the Holocaust, people who could have helped me understand that those horrors are part of *our* story, inwardly as well as outwardly. My teachers could have given me the critical tools necessary to connect the dots between the Holocaust, the Chicago suburbs, and myself.

When teachers intersect the "big story" with the "little story," personal issues will arise for teachers and students alike, but I am not proposing that we become unlicensed and unqualified therapists. Instead, I am proposing that we become better teachers. Teaching and learning, done well, are done not by disembodied intellects: they are done by whole persons whose intellects cannot be disentangled from the complex of faculties held together by the heart. As the neurobiologist Candace Pert has pointed out, the *brain* is located under the cranium, whereas the *mind* is distributed throughout the body.[13] To teach *as* a whole person *to* the whole person is not to lose one's professionalism; it is to take it to a deeper level.[14]

As we do so, we will serve democracy's cause by teaching habits of the heart that will, for example, help us avoid some of the personal and social pathologies that led to the Holocaust. We will help our students learn that the facts in every field—the history of cruelty and creativity, the degradation and restoration of the environment, the literature of despair and hope—pose tension-inducing questions that, if embraced, can make them better citizens *and* better people.[15]

Doing Democracy in School

If we want to teach democratic habits of the heart in our classrooms, we need to help our students explore their inner potential. At the same time we need to help them explore their outer potential—in the school community and in the larger civic community—drawing them into a live encounter with democracy in action.

The Holocaust was aided and abetted by a German system of higher education that hewed to the norms of "pure" scholarship and kept the life of the mind hermetically sealed off from the life of the world. This deprived Germany of sources of information and social criticism that might have helped mitigate evil. Worse still, it created an educated class trained to ignore the suffering happening in their own backyard who felt entitled to the luxury of selective ignorance.

The American approach to public education, with its focus on practical skills rather than pure scholarship, differs in theory from the Germanic approach. But our pedagogy has consequences reminiscent of the German model when it makes students into passive recipients of knowledge about subjects taught at arm's length. Students taught that way, as I was taught about the Holocaust, have a hard time connecting the world they have learned about with the world in which they live. They fail to develop the sense of curiosity, responsibility, and agency that citizenship requires.

It is especially ironic that many required civics classes fail to teach democratic habits of the heart. Our state standards for public education invariably contain strong rhetoric about the need to educate citizens. Too often that goal is implemented by requiring students to learn little more than key dates, names, documents, and events associated with American history, along with the basic structures and processes of institutional democracy.

This approach falls far short of our rhetorical goals, as educator Kimberly E. Koehler Freitag explains in an article focused on the state of Illinois:

> The introductory paragraph of the *Illinois Learning Standards for Social Science* (1997) states, "The study of social science helps people develop the ability to make informed and reasoned decisions for the public good as citizens of a culturally diverse, democratic society in an interdependent world." . . . A [close] examination of the document, however, reveals that the actual goals, learning standards and benchmarks will not result in students' developing decision-making skills. They will not help students to learn to define what constitutes the "public good" or an "interdependent world." The construct "democratic society" is treated as a function of its documents and government structures rather than as what [John] Dewey . . . described as ". . . primarily a mode of associated living, of conjoint communicated experience." Cultural diversity is treated in terms of artifacts of culture. [The] discrepancy between the lofty statement of purpose and the actual guidelines for practitioners [leads one to] conclude that the State of Illinois is not truly committed to the democratic ideals proclaimed in the document's introduction.[16]

Students need to learn basic data about the history and the structures of American democracy, of course. But if students are to be well served and are to serve democracy well, we need to invite them into a lived engagement with democracy's core concepts and values. There are at least two ways to do this: by engaging students in democratic processes within the classroom and the school and by involving them in the political dynamics of the larger community.

The need to practice democracy within the school, along with some guidance for doing it, has been articulated persuasively by Scott Nine, executive director of the Institute for Democratic Education in America:[17]

> If we expect our youth to become adults who exercise reflective judgment, [take] responsibility for themselves and their community, and . . . take part in shaping their country and its policies, then the environment in which they are schooled must teach them how to do that—it must give them practice in real responsibility, real dialogue, and real authority.

> Most students in school are treated as if they have no judgment at all, except around trivial, adult-constructed matters, and are given very little responsibility, except to "achieve." Then we expect them to transform into fully functioning members of a participatory democracy at the moment they turn eighteen. That's an inherent conflict, a problem that we can name. Meanwhile, the accelerating rate of economic, climate, technological, and social change makes concepts of student success into nuanced and moving targets that require significant remodeling of our prevailing public paradigms regarding education.

> Practices that give young people a voice in their own learning, that support their broad development including social, personal, and intellectual growth, and that connect [them] to their local community and the surrounding environment must find renewed life in and beyond the classroom. Student [advisers], mentoring, apprenticeships, restorative justice, self-managed learning, and shared governance practices can make tangible differences in a student's sense of belonging, autonomy, and mattering.

> Innovative instructional practices that utilize open-source technology, invite students to co-create lessons and texts, and see the student

more as a designer and less as a test-taker are vital to meet students' desires for competence. As the highly lauded teacher Anthony Armstrong says, "No one should be asking students questions they can easily Google to answer."

> We need our schools to become centers of community that are more equitable, more honest, more relevant, more welcoming, and more like places where real thinking happens. Our best educators know how to create these conditions, and they need our support and encouragement. Our best educators are classroom teachers, but not just teachers. Our best educators are also our plumbers, electricians, administrative assistants, construction foremen, and more. Our ability to reclaim our democracy will likely be rooted in the places we call school, key sites of social transformation, and in the new ways we can envision them and what learning looks like both inside and beyond classroom walls.[18]

No one who is thoughtful about this subject argues that a democratic education means teachers abdicating responsibility for framing and guiding a learning agenda, turning all such decisions over to popular vote. The challenge for teachers is to create a model of civic education that practices what it preaches—and to lead in the struggle to turn their schools into places that support that kind of education.[19]

Involving students with the community beyond the schoolhouse door has benefits that are now well known, thanks to the rise of service learning over the past several decades.[20] A case in point is the Youth Civic Engagement program in Hampton, Virginia.[21] Created in 1990 in collaboration with the public schools, its purpose was

> to instill community pride and leadership skills in young people and engage them in governance. The program was systematic, first fostering civic awareness through local service projects, then building collaboration and leadership skills through involvement with city boards and commissions on issues of increasing complexity. Young people contributed ideas—on better policing, school reform, job training—and helped with policy implementation.[22]

As I write, the twenty-year-old Hampton program is still running strong and has yielded long-term results on every level. The city's college-age youth "outperform peer groups in three key measures of citizenship: the ability to engage in civic discourse, passion for their community, and leadership skills." "Fewer families are fleeing the city, crime is down, and [the city's] voting rate is about twenty percent higher than similar communities." In 2007, "*Money* magazine rated the city as one of the 'Best Places to Live' in the U.S."[23] Service learning and related action-reflection programs not only help students grow as citizens but help communities grow as well.

An equally important and often neglected fact is that community engagement programs can enhance student learning of academic material. In a large political science class at a state university, three-fourths of the students, randomly selected, were assigned a normal syllabus. The remaining fourth were assigned all of that plus a service learning placement that required them to spend a few hours each week in the community.

One might think that the members of the latter group would do less well academically. After all, they had to spend extra time and energy on field assignments and might even have resented that fact. In fact, the students who were assigned to work in the community did *better* academically. Their out-of-school involvement made the bookwork more real and helped them become more deeply engaged with course materials.[24]

The Hidden Curriculum

The idea of the "hidden curriculum" is simple, self-evident, and widely ignored. Students learn not only from *what* is taught: they also learn from *how* it is taught. Students may take a course on democratic values that is full of solid information. But if the teacher does little more than dictate that information and then demand that students memorize and parrot it on tests, they are not learning democratic values.

Instead, they are learning to survive as subjects of an autocracy: keep your head down, your mouth shut, and repeat the party line whether or not you understand it or believe it.

The relational dynamics of the classroom have a more lasting impact on students than information that they retain just long enough to pass the test. Too many students spend long hours in classrooms where they are mere audience to a teacher's performance. They become passive recipients of expert knowledge rather than active participants in a process of inquiry, discovery, and co-creation. To say the obvious, this is poor preparation for citizenship: democracy is not a spectator sport in which citizens can sit back and watch the pros at work.

If we want to reform this pedagogy, we must understand its root system: education arises from a cult of expertise. Expertise itself is not the problem. Some people know more about certain things than other people do, and their knowledge is to be respected. The problem lies in that little word *cult*. When experts are given the "guru" voice, the only voice that counts—robbing everyone else of the right, the confidence, or even the impulse to speak—probing questions are stifled, dissenting voices are silenced, and the experts go unchallenged. We never hear from people who have deep experiential knowledge without benefit of expert credentials. We never learn how to hold tension creatively because there are no ambiguities, only claims of certainty, in the cult of expertise.

Cultic deference to the experts distorts the educational mission and undermines democracy. But the roots of this cult run deep, as deep as the rise of science itself, which is a fact full of irony. Let me be clear: I have profound respect for the methods and aims of science and for its many gifts to our common life. I have no wish to return to the days when the subjective "truth" of some powerful priest or potentate could cause such abominations as the burning of "witches."

The irony is that with the rise of science came a new class of priests and potentates: the scientists themselves. Very few scientists claim that kind of authority for themselves, but laypeople often project it on them. So the same science that allowed us to transcend a benighted culture

HEALING THE HEART OF DEMOCRACY

of subjective "truth," thus contributing to democracy, also created a popular mentality that supports the rise of autocracy: "I have no expert knowledge in this matter. I am told that there are those who do. So I will let the authorities make the decisions."

This is why it sometimes feels as if we had returned to the era of priests, potentates, and a passive populace—especially in our popular discourse about politics and economics, where false certainties repeated often and loudly enough by self-proclaimed "experts" are accepted by many people at face value. In this respect, the passivity shown by those who never question Fox News (whose regular viewers have been found to be the most misinformed about basic matters of fact), is no different from the passivity of those who never question the truth claims of academic elites.[25]

Given the mixed blessings of science, democracy is not well served when our schools are pressured to ramp up science education at the expense of the humanities, whose disciplines teach people to look at the world from unconventional angles and ask probing questions. Some of that pressure comes from the notion that the main purpose of education is to prepare students for a technological society where math and science are the only subjects that count. Some of it comes from the demand for educational accountability, which means teaching subjects whose outcomes are measurable. Graduating employable students is a worthy goal, but not when it is equated with math and science education. Holding educators accountable for results is another worthy goal, but not when it is equated with tallying up the number of facts students can memorize.

Both of these drivers create an educational bias against the humanities. For most students, courses in philosophy, literature, music, and the arts do not translate directly into jobs. And the most important outcomes of such courses are difficult to measure because they work at the subtle levels of human sensibility. But the humanities help form habits of the heart that are crucial to democracy's future—including humility, chutzpah, and the capacity to hold tension creatively—all of which help counter the cult of expertise.

The writer Mark Slouka makes the point succinctly and well:

> The case for the humanities is not hard to make. . . . The humanities, done right, are the crucible within which our evolving notions of what it means to be fully human are put to the test; they teach us, incrementally, endlessly, not what to do but how to be. Their method is confrontational, their domain unlimited, their "product" not truth but the reasoned search for truth. . . .
>
> They are thus, inescapably, political. Why? Because they complicate our vision, pull our most cherished notions out by the roots, flay our pieties. Because they grow uncertainty. Because they expand the reach of our understanding (and therefore our compassion), even as they force us to draw and redraw the borders of tolerance. Because out of all this work of self-building might emerge an individual capable of humility in the face of complexity; an individual formed through questioning and therefore unlikely to cede that right; an individual resistant to coercion, to manipulation and demagoguery in all their forms. The humanities, in short, are a superb delivery mechanism for what we might call democratic values. There is no better that I am aware of.[26]

As is true of any subject, *how* we teach the humanities is as important as *that* we teach them, and the humanities are no freer from the cult of expertise than the sciences are. Too many students learn about Socrates' dialogical method by hearing someone lecture about it instead of participating in it. Too many students study a great poem or novel through the lens of critical opinion instead of a personal engagement with the text. And too many students learn about the arts by studying famous artifacts instead of making art. When the cult of expertise converges with our mania for testing, it is hard to gain support for pedagogies that go beyond teaching the *what* of things into the labor-intensive process of teaching the *how* of things.

And yet, against all odds, that is exactly what we who care about democracy must do. Thomas Jefferson said, "I know of no safe repository of the ultimate power of society but people. And if we think them not enlightened enough, the remedy is not to take the power from them, but to inform them by education."[27] A man of action as well as reflection, who learned experientially as well as by reading great literature, Jefferson would surely agree that how we teach people to be trust holders of democracy is as important as what we teach them.

Congregations and Habits of the Heart

As I turn toward congregations as places where democratic habits of the heart can be formed, a few words about my personal religious perspective: I am a Christian raised in the mainline Protestant tradition that helped shape American culture and politics for about two hundred years, until the middle of the twentieth century, when its influence began to wane as the power of evangelical Christianity began to grow. As an adult, I became a Quaker, attracted to Quakerism's respect for the "inner teacher," its appreciation of human diversity, its way of holding tension (as in the John Woolman story), and its spiritually grounded social activism.

For many years, I have been a participant in and a student of American religious life. I have good reason to appreciate the contributions that religion has made to the commonweal *and* to fear certain forms of religious passion. My core religious beliefs include this simple article of faith: the God who gave all of us life wants us to do the same for each other. When people or groups who claim religious motivation make their points by using violence in any form—spiritual, psychological, verbal, or physical—it seems clear to me that they are driven by fear rather than faith, committed to control instead of trust in God.

The writer Anne Lamott says, "You can safely assume you've created God in your own image when it turns out that God hates all the same people you do."[28] Lamott makes me laugh even as I acknowledge with sadness that she accurately describes what some believers do, despite scriptural injunctions against idolatry.

The sacred texts of all the major religious traditions say, in effect, "God loves everyone and you should, too." The British religion scholar

Karen Armstrong offers a synopsis of this core principle in the opening paragraph of her well-known "Charter of Compassion":

> The principle of compassion lies at the heart of all religious, ethical and spiritual traditions, calling us always to treat all others as we wish to be treated ourselves. Compassion impels us to work tirelessly to alleviate the suffering of our fellow creatures, to dethrone ourselves from the centre of our world and put another there, and to honour the inviolable sanctity of every single human being, treating everybody, without exception, with absolute justice, equity and respect.[29]

Good words in good books are important. They allow us to call ourselves and each other back when we go astray, as when John Woolman used Quaker rhetoric to call his faith community back to its truth. But words in books are not enough; if they were, there would not be so much straying. Religious leaders who want to teach the habits of the heart that make democracy possible—not least the habit called compassion—often find they must transform the hidden curriculum of congregational life, those relational dynamics that have more impact on parishioners than preaching and teaching the articles of faith.

At a Quaker meeting I once attended, a poster at the front of the meeting room posed a question that illustrates what I mean by relational dynamics: "Do we trust sufficiently in the goodwill of our members to make our needs and concerns known?" In the mainline Protestant tradition I grew up in, the honest answer is often no. I have talked with many parishioners who regard personal relationships in their congregations as unsafe when it comes to exploring sensitive personal issues.

If they were to speak, for example, of a marriage gone awry, a failure at work, or a substance abuse problem, they fear possibilities ranging from damaging gossip to subtle forms of shunning to judgment and rejection. They fear the failure of compassion in practice despite the words found in their own Scriptures and creeds. So instead of turning to members of the congregation for understanding and support, they seek confidential counseling in the privacy of the pastor's office or from a professional outside of their church. Many religious communities have a long way to go when it comes to embodying their verbal commitment to compassion among their own members, let alone in the larger world.

What I know about the low level of trust in some Protestant churches is helpful when clergy ask me to help their "homogenous white congregations" embrace more of the diversity that characterizes our society. They rightly feel indicted by a line that Martin Luther King Jr. frequently used in his sermons: "Eleven o'clock Sunday morning is the most segregated hour in America, and Sunday school is still the most segregated school of the week."[30]

My response to the requests I get to help such congregations "diversify" is simple: "There is no such thing as a 'homogenous white congregation.' There are only groups of white people pretending that they have no critical differences among themselves for fear that their 'community' would crumble if they opened their real lives to one another. Why would anyone with a *visible* difference want to join a group of people who look like each other but cannot embrace their own *invisible* differences?"

The question for congregations that want to help members develop democratic habits of the heart goes well beyond asking, "What words in our sacred texts are we called to live by?" The deeper, more demanding question is, "How can we create relationships among us that bring those words to life, ways of being together that are congruent with what we teach and preach?"

When a worshiping community develops embodied answers to those questions, its lived witness becomes a draw far more powerful than any doctrine or text. As the first-century theologian Tertullian observed, strangers in the ancient world—who had been conditioned by their culture to distrust and despise one another—had one compelling reason to join the early Christian church. As they looked in on those small gatherings of people who were once strangers to each other, they were astonished to "see how they love one another."[31]

Parishioners will become more compassionate toward democracy's diversity as they become more compassionate toward the diversity within their own ranks. There are many ways to help that happen, to help community emerge within the institutional structures of religious life; I will explore some of them in a moment. But before the hidden curriculum of lived relationships can be aligned with the words of our sacred texts, we must examine the prevailing pattern of authority within congregational life. As we do, we often discover that we can make little progress toward a community of compassion until we change that pattern.

Who's in Charge Here?

When a congregation is profoundly clergy-centered—when the pedagogy consists of a clergyperson (performer) downloading information and inspiration to parishioners (audience)—the game is rigged. The theological message may be one of community, but the lived experience is one of dependence on an authority. Under those conditions, not much can be done to build the communal trust that allows compassion to flower, no matter how benign the leader is.

Of course, certain religious traditions are deeply committed to a hierarchical model of authority on principle: their primary goal is not to create community but to enforce doctrinal unity. Even in nonhierarchical traditions, some clergy still play their role in an autocratic manner, for reasons that range from their theological convictions about who is qualified to represent God to their personal need for control.

However, every tradition has many clergy who want—and are willing to work for—a more participatory form of congregational life. They are eager to draw members into various forms of communal engagement that go beyond pledging money and serving on committees. They want to help people learn to think theologically about their own experience and find their own voices on matters of faith and life.

And yet these leaders often encounter the same sort of resistance from parishioners that teachers face when they try to draw students into a learning community. Many laypeople are reluctant to speak for themselves on religious matters, preferring instead to have the trained and ordained leader "do their religion" for them. They may even become resentful when clergy invite them to become, in effect, leaders of the congregation. "After all," they think, "we are paying this person to lead us on a journey of faith, not to ask us what direction we think we should go."

How well a leader deals with this resistance depends heavily on how well he or she diagnoses its causes. Laypeople who want the clergy to do it all (like their student counterparts) are not, for the most part, lazy, dependent, or ignorant. Instead, their voices have been diminished by the same cult of expertise that diminishes students in classrooms. They have been conditioned to believe that they have nothing worth saying about things theological, which professionals often discuss in terms so arcane that an amateur cannot decode them. Laypeople, like students, suffer from a wound inflicted by a culture that fails to help them find their voices. The preacher or teacher who wants true community must be committed to helping people find a voice that they are often unaware they have lost.

Again, I do not discount expert knowledge. In my stream of the Christian tradition, many people have been liberated by scholarly knowledge about how the Bible was written and how our theology was formed. These are historical processes of great complexity that were influenced as much by culture and politics as by spiritual forces: laypeople need to be taught, and taught well, for the sake of full understanding. But the teacher who makes these complexities accessible to the laity must also ask questions of them: "Now that you understand where this passage or faith claim comes from, what do you make of it? What does it say to you about your own experience? And what do you want to say back to it—and to us—on the basis of your experiential knowledge?"

The leader or teacher who wants to work this way needs at least two deep-rooted habits of the heart: patience and self-confidence. It is hard to try to liberate people's voices only to hear them say, silently or aloud, "Stop asking us all these questions—you are not doing your job! Just tell us what we are supposed to think, believe, and do about all this." Those of us who want to lead people toward a stronger sense of voice and agency must have a well-developed capacity for tension-holding so that we can stand the gaff long enough to free first one, then another, and then another layperson to say, however hesitantly, "OK, here's what I think."

As that kind of speaking multiplies, laypeople will hear things from each other that they disagree with, things that may cause consternation for people accustomed to hearing only the voice of the leader. How better to learn democratic habits of the heart such as listening openly and responding respectfully? And how better to learn them well than to see them modeled by a teacher who gracefully makes a space in which all voices are heard and honored?

As the leader consistently holds safe space where everyone's voice can be heard, a learning community begins to form in which people have a chance to develop that mix of humility and chutzpah on which democracy depends. As that community grows stronger, laypeople can return to their everyday lives with a new understanding of how faith informs their experience and experience informs their faith. But if this kind of community fails to form within a congregation, there can be no "ministry of the laity"—a concept that, rightly understood, is the religious equivalent of a "government of the people, by the people, for the people."

Power and Potluck Suppers

When authority is shared and the seeds of community have been planted, much can be done to bring a congregation's relational dynamics into alignment with words like *compassion*, to deepen hospitality within the religious community so that parishioners can become bearers of hospitality in the public world. Here are a few of them.

Years ago, when I began working as a community organizer in a community adjacent to Washington, D.C., I learned about a large black Baptist church that made major contributions to community well-being in a poverty-stricken and crime-ridden part of town. Eager for guidance, I went to see the pastor and asked him, in essence, "What is your secret?" I was hoping that this master of the trade would instruct me in the state-of-the-art theories and techniques of community organizing. Instead, he simply smiled and said, "Potluck suppers."

This is, of course, a secret hidden in plain sight: breaking bread together is one of the best ways to create community, a celebrated sacrament in the Christian church. In this Baptist congregation, potluck suppers were often held before and after various community actions, such as canvassing residents about community needs, sending a delegation to talk with city officials, or marching to protest an injustice or rally people to a cause. These suppers usually had a brief agenda focused on questions that would help attendees reflect on the issue at hand, but that was not their primary purpose. More important was the chance they gave parishioners to catch up with each other's lives and to tell personal and public stories that ranged from painful to hopeful to joyful, stories that create solidarity and energize action, helping people reweave relationships within the church for the sake of their ministry in the world.

As parishioners discovered the power of breaking bread around matters of shared concern, they began convening potlucks for people within and beyond the congregation who differed on difficult topics. For example, this congregation, like many, included parents of school-aged children and public school educators. These two groups sometimes found themselves at odds: parents felt that the schools were not giving their children what they needed, and educators felt that the parents were shirking their responsibilities for educating their own children. By exploring this sensitive issue in the context of a potluck supper, the dialogue was made more generous and generative than what often goes on at school board meetings where political outrage and posturing easily become the norm.

A similar transformation can occur when members of a congregation break bread with folks in the larger community with whom they have troubled relationships. In the neighborhood served by this Baptist church, for example, police-community relationships were continually under strain. The police were on high alert because of the high crime rate, and citizens were on high alert because of occasional police overreaction and even brutality. Over a series of potluck dialogues, church members and police created an early version of the community policing model whose effectiveness has led more and more communities to adopt it over the past twenty years.[32]

Potluck suppers can also help us deal with less visible societal wounds. In recent years, for example, some congregations have hosted powerful and healing dialogues between veterans and civilians.[33] From Vietnam onward, many vets have felt vilified by citizens who opposed the war in which they fought and misunderstood by citizens who supported the war but have no battlefield experience. The silence surrounding all of this has resulted in veterans being bitter about the ingratitude of the nation for which they fought, the low level of active citizen support for physical and mental health services for returning soldiers, and the indifference of many Americans to the fact that veterans constitute at least one-quarter of all homeless people in this country.

Open and honest conversations in a setting of deep hospitality, held as an ongoing program in a congregation, can plant seeds of healing and civic unity around this and other contentious and painful issues of our time. When a meal between conflicted parties begins with everyone bringing food to share, the silent subtext of the conversation is "We have the capacity to care for one another and collaborate toward a common good."

Decision Making and Counseling

Congregations perform two other functions that can help people develop democratic habits of the heart: making communal decisions and providing personal counseling. I have written about both of these elsewhere, at length.[34] Here I will simply offer a few pointers toward the possibilities.

Like all voluntary associations, congregations must make decisions that range from the mundane ("Should we repair the roof?") to those that raise complex personal and theological issues ("Should we bless same-sex marriages?"). There are at least two ways for groups to make decisions: majority rule and consensus. Majority rule is the only feasible method when the group is large. But most congregations are small enough that consensus is a realistic option, and even large congregations can seek consensus in small subgroups before the vote is taken.

When we make decisions by majority rule, we set up a win-lose contest. If the outcome is important to me, I listen to you first to determine whether we are on the same side. If I learn that we are not, I listen to what you say for everything that I regard as mistaken or misguided, screening out whatever I may agree with. Then I speak, proposing my superior solution while calling attention to your wrongheadedness. The ground rules of this contest compel us to become adversarial listeners and speakers, ratcheting up the tension between us and making it less bearable, which is why someone usually "calls the vote" long before the issue has been thoroughly explored.

When we make decisions by consensus, we cannot proceed as long as even one person feels obligated to object on practical or moral grounds.[35] Now I listen more openly to what you have to say—listen for where I might join with you and what I might learn from our differences—because I know we cannot move forward unless we move together. When I rise to speak, I am much more likely to try to bridge our positions than I am to strike down your viewpoint. We become collaborative listeners and speakers who develop democratic habits of the heart—such as speaking one's truth openly and listening to others respectfully—habits that can make our political discourse less divisive.

When we make decisions by consensus, we are not allowed to "resolve" conflict prematurely by choosing one thing or another. Instead we are required to hold the tension until it has a chance to open us to a larger synthesis. This requires patience, of course, but the rewards are considerable. Not only are we likely to be drawn toward a resolution better than anything we envisioned at the outset, but in the process, we also deepen our sense of community instead of splitting into subgroups of satisfied winners and disgruntled losers.

Naturally, results come more slowly when we proceed by consensus. Critics often claim that we face issues of such urgency that patiently holding the tension before we make a decision is inefficient at best and irresponsible at worst. Whenever I hear that criticism, I tell the story of John Woolman that I related in Chapter I. Then I ask the critic if it was "inefficient" to get eighty years ahead of the Emancipation Proclamation on what is arguably the most urgent moral issue in American history.

The second function performed by most congregations is personal counseling for parishioners who seek help. By and large that help does not come from the community itself—it is available only in the privacy of the clergyperson's office. Clearly, there are problems so fraught and people so fragile that private sessions with a pastoral counselor are the best or only answer. And yet not all problems are that fraught and not all people are that fragile.

When a congregation says, in effect, "No matter who you are or what kind of problem you have, the only way to explore it is in strict confidentiality with a professional," the message may be unintended, but it is clear: "Members of this community do not have the resources to help each other negotiate life's challenges. And if you share your problems with fellow parishioners, you cannot be assured of confidentiality but you make yourself vulnerable to gossip."

A self-fulfilling prophecy is at work here, of course. As long as congregations lack options for communal counseling, the mutual trust and resourcefulness required to perform this function will remain in short supply because no one is given a chance to develop or practice them. This sounds like a vicious circle, but it can be broken. I have long personal experience with a well-tested method that has a proven capacity to create safe space for *some* parishioners to bring *some* problems to *some* of their fellow parishioners, even in congregations that have never had such a practice.

The Quaker process known as the clearness committee is a classic illustration of necessity's being the mother of invention. As a religious community that has no ordained clerical leaders, Quakers cannot take their problems into the privacy of the pastor's office. If members of Quaker meetings are to get help with personal issues, it must come from the community. In the clearness committee, five or six members of the meeting, chosen with care for their trustworthiness, sit with a so-called focus person who is wrestling with a problem, with the intent of helping the person gain clarity about how to deal with it.[36]

Crucial to the success of this process—which is surrounded by strict confidentiality—is that committee members understand and abide by ground rules that I have described at length in *A Hidden Wholeness*.[37] These rules center on two covenants, both based on the belief that every person has an "inner teacher"—a soul-deep source of whatever truth the person needs to hear and the best possible source of counsel in challenging times:

- Committee members will make no effort to "fix," advise, "save," or correct the focus person. Indeed, they will not speak to the focus person in any way except to ask honest, open questions.
- The questions asked will have one purpose only: to help the focus person have a deepening conversation not with members of the committee but with his or her inner teacher.

The ground rules of a clearness committee are easy to articulate but difficult to follow. The people involved must be committed to the process and well prepared for it—which includes learning how to ask honest, open questions and practicing the various forms of patience and restraint that make safe space for the vulnerable soul.

The time and energy this requires is rewarded on many levels. In the non-Quaker congregations I know where this process is offered as an alternative to private pastoral counseling—congregations whose leaders are willing to share that role and whose members are willing to take it up—people receive help with their personal dilemmas. Equally important, they form habits of the heart that help them develop a sense of resourcefulness, rebuild mutual trust, and revitalize the religious community, all of which serve the cause of democracy well.

A Theology of Hospitality

Earlier in this chapter, I focused on the word *compassion* and how we need to take it beyond religious rhetoric to make it an embodied habit of the heart. As I bring this chapter to a close, I want to focus on *hospitality,* another word close to the heart of all the major world religions and another habit of the heart vital to democracy.

Historically, habits of the heart have been shaped in part by the physical environment in which people found themselves. White American pioneers—who found themselves in a land with abundant food, water, and building materials almost everywhere they went—prided themselves on being self-sufficient, a virtue Americans have claimed as a national trait ever since. But Christianity and Judaism, America's dominant religious traditions, all began in the harsh deserts of the Middle East, as did Islam. Nomads in that trackless, treeless terrain must often depend on others for shelter and sustenance.

In the desert, people come to understand that the hospitality urged upon them by the sacred texts of all the Abrahamic traditions is not only a God-given norm but also a practical necessity. The pioneers of these traditions did not need to be exhorted to receive strangers with hospitality. They kept weaving and reweaving the fabric of hospitality because they knew that if the fabric failed, they would sooner or later perish in body as well as soul: today's generous host will be tomorrow's needy guest.

The American tradition of self-sufficiency is hard to overcome, though a moment's thought reveals it to be an illusion: even in a land of plenty, there is no way to do it all alone. Still, the message of interdependence is a hard sell in a consumer society where "buy what you need" is the norm and the culture of sharing is weak. And yet religious communities have a chance to help believers understand that in the absence of active hospitality, there is no such thing as a spiritual life.

The pivotal stories in the sacred texts of the traditions that I know best point to hospitable habits of the heart as a necessity, not an option, for people on a spiritual journey.* Here are brief sketches of two of them.

• Genesis 18 tells the story of Abraham and Sarah, who are well into their old age when they make camp in the desert at Mamre. Three strangers approach, and this elderly couple, rather than respond in fear, offer them food and drink. The strangers turn out to be angels of the Lord who make the startling announcement that Sarah, despite her advanced age, will bear a child. That child turns out to be Isaac, who comes to play a pivotal role as the second patriarch of the Jewish people and heir of the land of Israel, which he received from his father Abraham, the first patriarch.

• Luke 24 tells the story of two of Jesus's apostles walking down the road to Emmaus after the crucifixion. A stranger comes along and asks why they are so downcast. The apostles ask if he is the only visitor to Jerusalem who does not know what happened. The stranger calls them foolish for failing to believe the prophecies about Jesus, but the apostles are not reassured. As they get close to home, they urge the stranger to eat with them. Over supper their eyes are opened to the fact that this stranger is the risen Christ: "He was known to them in the breaking of the bread."

The moral of both stories is clear: when a believer fails to offer hospitality to the stranger, the spiritual journey comes to a sudden

*I regret that I do not know the Qur'an well enough to recount a parallel story from its pages. But Islam's sacred texts are full of exhortations to hospitality. Here is a famous Islamic Hadith, a narration concerning the words and deeds of the Prophet Muhammad: "Narrated Abu Shuraih Al-Adawi: My ears heard and my eyes saw the Prophet when he spoke, 'Anybody who believes in Allah and the Last Day, should serve his neighbor generously, and anybody who believes in Allah and the Last Day should serve his guest generously.'"

halt. Had Abraham and Sarah failed to offer hospitality, they could not have played their key roles as the agents of God's promise to the Jewish people. Had the disciples on the road to Emmaus failed to offer hospitality, they could not have played their key roles as bearers of the "good news" and founders of the early church.

Morals such as these are easily translated into secular language for nonbelievers: the stranger is someone who may come bearing news we need to know, news that will enlarge and enliven our world and alert us to possibilities that we would otherwise miss. Hospitality brings gifts to the host as well as to the guest—the gift of information that we would otherwise lack and the gift of feeling more at home in a world full of strangers.

Becoming people who offer hospitality to strangers requires us to open our hearts time and again to the tension created by our fear of "the other." That is why many wisdom traditions highlight the creative possibilities of a heart broken open instead of apart. Only from such a heart can hospitality flow—toward the stranger and toward all that we find alien and unsettling.

In Christian tradition, the broken-open heart is virtually indistinguishable from the image of the cross. It was on the cross that God's heart was broken for the sake of humankind, broken open into a love that Christ's followers are called to emulate. Even as a physical form, the cross—with arms that stretch left and right and up and down—symbolizes the tension, the "excruciating" tension, that can open the heart to love.

For Jews, learning to live openheartedly in the face of immense and devastating heartbreak is a historical as well as spiritual imperative. So it is no surprise that Jewish teaching includes frequent reminders of the importance of a broken-open heart, as in this Hasidic tale:

> A disciple asks the rebbe: "Why does Torah tell us to 'place these words *upon* your hearts'? Why does it not tell us to place these holy words *in* our hearts?" The rebbe answers: "It is because as we are, our hearts are closed, and we cannot place the holy words in our hearts.

So we place them on top of our hearts. And there they stay until, one day, the heart breaks and the words fall in."[38]

Secular humanism does not speak explicitly of a heart broken open to "otherness," and yet the essence of that idea is laced through this ancient and honorable tradition. Humanism urges us to develop intellectual habits that allow us to hold the tension of opposites without coming undone. So a liberal education, which emerges from the heart of the humanistic tradition, emphasizes the ability to look at an issue from all sides, to be comfortable with contradictions and ambiguities, and to honor paradox in thought, speech, and action. Humanism helps us let the tension of opposites open us to new insight.

In the end, the challenge faced by adherents of every tradition of faith or reason is the same one we face in our public lives: to let the stranger—and things we find strange—be who and what they are, allowing them to open us to the vexing and enlivening mysteries we find within and around us. Whether our Ultimate Reality is God or Reason, fear constantly tempts us to try to tame it and contain it within the boundaries of our own comfort zones. Doing so dishonors the Ultimate, diminishes the scope of our lives, and keeps us from developing a key habit of the heart that democracy requires.

If religious communities could help believers develop the kind of courageous hospitality described by the poet Rainer Maria Rilke, they would serve themselves, their traditions, and the imperatives of democracy well:

> This is at bottom the only courage that is demanded of us: to have courage for the most strange, the most singular, and the most inexplicable that we may encounter. That humankind has in this sense been cowardly has done life endless harm; the experiences that are called "visions," the whole so-called "spirit-world," death and all those things that are so closely akin to us have, by daily parrying, been so crowded out of life that the senses by which we could have grasped them are atrophied. To say nothing of God.[39]

[CHAPTER VII]

Safe Space for Deep Democracy

You must have a room, or a certain hour or so a day, where you don't know what was in the newspapers that morning . . . a place where you can simply experience and bring forth what you are and what you might be.

—JOSEPH CAMPBELL, *The Power of Myth*[1]

Democratic action depends upon . . . free spaces, where people experience a schooling in citizenship and learn a vision of the common good in the course of struggling for change.

—SARA EVANS AND HARRY BOYTE, *Free Spaces*[2]

In the last two chapters, I explored the way we develop habits of the heart in spaces such as classrooms, houses of worship, and the many venues of public life. But the spaces in which our hearts are formed are not always made of bricks and mortar—they are also created by images, ideas, and ideals. These are not places with street addresses but invisible conceptual or notional spaces that we can take with us wherever we go.

As Alexis de Tocqueville pointed out, the founders' ideal of "life, liberty and the pursuit of happiness" created a conceptual space that all Americans inhabited, whether they lived in the heart of a city or on the far frontier. It was a democratic space that freed up innovative energies unknown in Tocqueville's France, where imperial fears of popular uprisings led to strict limits on the size and content of public gatherings.[3]

The notional spaces that liberate or limit us do not always come from external dictates. They come from within us as well, and carry at least as much clout as any external command. If I harbor racist notions, for example, I create a portable prison that keeps me apart from "them." A space charged with hatred imposes limits on my life, depriving me of any chance to learn what I have in common with "the other" or how our differences might enrich me. If, on the other hand, I embrace notions of shared humanity, I go through the day in a portable space that energizes me to interact with people of all kinds, enlarging my life and allowing me to help reweave the civic community as I go.

The wellspring of all notional space is the human heart. That is why Terry Tempest Williams calls the heart the "first home of democracy,"[4] the place where we wrestle with democracy's basic questions, emerging with answers on which so much depends. If our hearts are large and supple enough to hold the tensions of those questions in a life-giving way, they produce ideas and ideals that feed a living democracy. If our hearts are so small and brittle that they implode or explode under tension, they produce "ideals" like Aryan supremacy and "ideas" like the Nazis' *Endlösung*, their chilling "final solution."

This heart-source is invisible, but the impact of what flows from it is visible everywhere. It is seen in moments of horror when we rally "our kind" to kill off "the other" with weapons that range from disrespect to genocide. It is seen in moments of grace when we transcend our differences and work together on behalf of the common good. In this chapter I will explore some of the notional or conceptual spaces in which our habits of the heart are formed, invisible spaces where democracy visibly lives or dies.

When the Media Define Reality

The most consequential conceptual space that most of us inhabit when it comes to politics is the space defined by the media. We are continually surrounded—in print, over the airwaves, and online—by a "blooming, buzzing confusion" of information, disinformation, infotainment, and opinion that presents itself as information.[5] And almost all of it is generated by media controlled by a handful of megacorporations.

As a result, most of us do not live in a real-life political space but in a media-generated caricature or cartoon of such a space. I am not suggesting that the media are all bad or that we do not need the best of them. Ignorance is the death knell of democracy, and we can hear that bell tolling today: it is disconcerting to learn that while 73 percent of Americans can name the Three Stooges, only 42 percent can name the three branches of government.[6] Good citizens need the information that comes from a mix of reliable sources.

But when we give the media exclusive rights to define our political world, we are almost certain to end up with a distorted sense of reality and deformed habits of the heart. Let me count the ways:

• The media portray our problems at such a rapid pace and on such a massive scale that we are discouraged from even trying to get leverage on them. Instead of providing empowerment for citizens to act, the pace and scale of news coverage leads to information overload and retreat into private life.

• Most media portray complex events and issues using highly selective images and sound bites, rarely allowing the extended exploration that an understanding of reality requires.

• The media tend to highlight the latest malfeasance, scandal, or tragedy. They know that bad news sells better than good news, so that is what they sell—despite the fact that it gives us an unbalanced picture of the complex mix of darkness and light in the world.

• The media pander to our short attention spans, thereby intensifying them. Last week's hot story—which will continue to be important to the people directly involved for months and years to come—is erased from our awareness by this week's big news.

• The media focus on suffering, replaying it time and again, rarely helping us understand its sources and, when they do, sometimes misplacing the blame. Saturated with suffering, we either become numbed to it or turn away feeling overwhelmed. And if we work through those feelings and want to address the suffering at its source, the media tend to direct us to the wrong places.

• The visual media can create the illusion that we have "been there and seen it all"—to a war zone, a crime-ridden neighborhood, or a political rally—when in fact we have not. If the media become our only eyes to the world, it is hard to convince us that what we have "seen with our own eyes" may not be entirely true.

• The few megacorporations that own a large share of the media often put their economic and political agendas ahead of good journalism, which drives some journalists to report whatever sells, committed to keeping their jobs rather than to doing them well.

Of course, "We the People" share the blame for this situation—we create the market for what the media are selling. We want our news in bite-size nuggets that fit our short attention spans; we are drawn to the latest disaster or scandal like gawkers at a highway crash; we like the illusion that we have been there when in fact we have not; many of us trust only the sources that square with our own opinions and beliefs; we are addicted to the high we get from hot rhetoric and gross exaggeration; if we become numbed or overwhelmed, we have an excuse for not being engaged; and some of us would prefer to live vicariously via celebrities and scandals instead of being involved with real-world issues in our own lives. We are the ideal customers for a product that contains toxins harmful to democracy's health.[7]

Again, we need the information that reliable media can provide us. But when Joseph Campbell said that we "must have a room, or a certain hour or so a day" where we "don't know what was in the newspapers that morning," he named an equally important need, one that becomes more pressing every day.[8] If we are to be citizens of a democracy, we must spend time in conceptual spaces defined by personal experience, not by the mass media, spaces where we can get the news that comes from within.

If we fail to turn inward for some of our news, we cannot embrace the questions that Terry Tempest Williams names as those on which democracy depends—questions about our inner capacity for mutual respect, generosity, listening openly to others, courage, trust, and resolve.[9] Those questions require constant self-examination and frequent self-correction. If we hold them honestly and well, we are more likely to carry safe space for democracy within us as we enter external spaces where democracy's conflicts and tensions are found.

Getting the News from Within

With his counsel that everyone needs "a place where you can simply experience and bring forth what you are and what you might be," Joseph Campbell highlights the importance of a "portable monastic cell" if we are to hold democracy's questions honestly and well. The writer and literary critic William Deresiewicz puts Campbell's point in historical context when he says, "Without solitude—the solitude of Adams and Jefferson and Hamilton and Madison and Thomas Paine—there would be no America."[10]

It is worth noting that Deresiewicz's comment came from a 2009 address, not to academics or monks but to West Point cadets. He argued that the frenetic multitasking that helped get these young men and women into West Point will not serve them or their troops well when they become military officers in life-and-death situations. Leadership of that sort requires a person to become a reflective practitioner, which means developing the capacity to be alone in dialogue with one's own soul.

The same is true of being good citizens in a frenzied world. Once a day, we might lock the door to our home or office, turn off our digital devices, put down our work, quiet ourselves inwardly as well as outwardly, and reflect for a while on what is moving within us. As this practice deepens, we learn that becoming a monk every now and then does not mean detaching from the world but entering more deeply into it. The news of the world—all of it, hellish and heavenly—begins in the heart. The better we know our own hearts, the better we know our world.

A story about Thomas Merton, Trappist monk and writer, provides a case in point. In 1944, Merton entered a Trappist monastery in the woods of Kentucky to live a walled-off life of radical solitude, silence, and prayer. He began to write books on the inner life, including *Seeds of Contemplation,* which was widely read and admired. Then, in 1964, he shocked his pious audience by publishing *Seeds of Destruction,* in which he predicted the spread of violent racial conflict in the United States several years before Martin Luther King Jr. was assassinated and the cities began to burn.

When *Seeds of Destruction* came out, with its prophecy of "the fire next time," Merton was taken to task by Martin Marty, a well-known theologian and urban activist who reviewed the book. Marty said, in effect, "How dare this cloistered monk hiding out in the woods tell those of us on the front lines that the racial problems we are working hard to solve are going to blow up in our faces?"

Three years later, in 1967, as Merton's prophecy came true, Marty wrote an open letter to Merton in the *National Catholic Reporter,* apologizing "for having put down" *Seeds of Destruction.* With most of the summer of 1967 past, he said, it is now evident "that you were correct."[11]

> What bothers me now is the degree of accuracy in your predictions
> and prophecies in general. At the time [that I published my criticism]
> you seemed to be trying to be a white James Baldwin. Now it seems
> to me that you were "telling it as it is" and maybe "as it will be."[12]

The data that gave Merton his deep insight into the dynamics of race in the United States came not from radio and television reports or the buzz on the streets; he was far removed from all such sources. Instead, Merton read Scripture, social criticism, fiction, and poetry. He corresponded with trusted friends. He read the black poets and listened to African American music, especially jazz and blues. Most important, he explored his inner life as a privileged white male human being. Through contemplative practice, he went to an inner space where the media cannot take us, a space where truth has a chance to come clear.

What gave Merton his prophetic eye was the insight into the human condition that he found within himself—including an understanding of the way white privilege maintains itself by denying or diminishing the reality of oppression. This is a hard truth for a white person to hear under any circumstance. And yet it is easier to hear it in the ego-shattering silence and solitude of the monastery than amid the self-important static of the larger world where we too often depend on ego energy to keep us going.

By listening with care to his own heart—and to the news contained in the poetic and musical voices of the oppressed—Merton saw that assurances of justice coming from white activists masked a deeper, unconscious struggle. He saw this more clearly than the activists did, blinded as we all can be by the ego investments that accompany our activism, by our insistence that we can accomplish whatever we set out to do. If we don't know our own story well, in its darkness as well as its light, we cannot know the story of "the other" in its fullness. And if we cannot empathize imaginatively with other people's stories, how much can we know about the real news of the world?

In his 1968 book *Conjectures of a Guilty Bystander*, in a passage inspired by the Quaker philosopher Douglas Steere, Merton writes about the way well-intended activists can become so ensnared in their commitments that they lose clarity, composure, and true self, which leads them to commit unintentional violence:

> There is a pervasive form of modern violence to which the idealist . . . most easily succumbs: activism and overwork. The rush and pressure of modern life are a form, perhaps the most common form, of its innate violence. To allow oneself to be carried away by a multitude of conflicting concerns, to surrender to too many demands, to commit oneself to too many projects, to want to help everyone in everything is to succumb to violence. The frenzy of the activist neutralizes his

work. . . . It destroys the fruitfulness of his own work, because it kills the root of inner wisdom which makes work fruitful.[13]

From Solitude to Circles of Trust

Merton's story is instructive, to a point. We need safe spaces, silent and solitary spaces, where we can get the news from within. But when it comes to forming the habits of the heart that make a democracy work, solitude has its limits. We also need safe spaces for small gatherings of the "company of strangers," spaces where citizens can come together to explore the challenge of living heartfelt lives in the neighborhood, in the workplace, and in the larger world.

Fortunately, such spaces exist, spaces where we can reclaim, exercise, and open our hearts in the company of others. As we gather in them, we will find ourselves better able to connect with one another and make creative use of democracy's tensions. I make these claims with confidence because for the past twenty years I have been working with a growing number of colleagues to create spaces of this sort for people across the country through a nonprofit organization called the Center for Courage & Renewal.[14]

The Center's mission is to "nurture personal and professional integrity and the courage to act on it" by means of what we call the Circle of Trust approach.[15] These circles typically involve twenty to twenty-five people who journey together in facilitated programs and retreats, frequently over the course of a year or more. At the time of this writing, we have worked directly with nearly forty thousand people from many walks of life: public school teachers and leaders, college professors and administrators, physicians and other health care providers, business and nonprofit leaders, clergy and lay leaders, attorneys, and philanthropists. All of them came to the Center's programs driven by a desire to "rejoin soul and role" in the workplace—one of the key venues in which habits of the heart are formed—where these people affect the lives of the hundreds of thousands of people whom they serve.[16]

I wrote about circles of trust at length in *A Hidden Wholeness*, and information about the Center's programs—including programs related to democracy and habits of the heart—is available at its Web site. So I will not go into detail here about the theory and practice that informs our circles. Instead, I want to tell a story about how such circles, and similar processes, can help us find the courage to confront conditions that compromise our deepest values and use the energy of that tension to help transform our part of the world.[17]

In a circle I facilitated for physicians, one man seemed especially burdened. For the first four sessions of this three-day retreat, he did not speak, though he was clearly paying close attention to what others had to say, much of which involved value conflicts at work. At some point in the fifth session, I said to the group, "Let's settle into a time of silence. Then I invite you to speak your truth from your own center into the center of the circle. Please speak *from* yourself *to* the space between us, not in response to what someone else has said."

After a while, the silent physician found his voice, speaking slowly and simply, the way people do when they are trying to tell a hard truth: "The regulations of the health care system where I work have me on the edge of violating my Hippocratic Oath two or three times a week." Those words hung in the air for a while as everyone followed circle of trust practices such as trusting the silence and not responding with either cheerleading or criticism. Then he spoke again: "I've never said that to any of my professional peers." There was more silence, and he spoke a third time: "The truth is, this is the first time I've said that to myself."

The import of this moment was not lost on anyone. We had just seen a person dive deep into his own truth, resurfacing to share what he had found down there with others *and* with himself. We had seen a person embrace a life-threatening contradiction—spiritually life-threatening for him and physically for his patients—between his deepest commitments and the demands of his workplace. He had named a tension that would continue to demand his attention and might just change his life. But instead of trying to walk around it, he walked right into the middle of it.

This small story has large implications for the kinds of safe spaces we need to help people develop democratic habits of the heart—especially the habit of creative tension-holding—that can transform our workplaces *and* our public and political lives. What conditions were established in this circle of trust that allowed this critical moment of truth-telling to occur?

Everything we do in these circles is informed by the assumption that all of us have an inner teacher who wants to tell us the truth. Most of us have difficulty hearing that voice for at least two reasons: the noise around us and the noise within us. In our retreats, we do what we can to turn off all of that noise and gather in a space that is as hospitable to silence as it is to honest speech.

The words that arise from this silence are evoked by questions of meaning and purpose, the only kind that interest the inner teacher—questions that help us explore the connections between our inner and outer lives. We set those questions in the context provided by poems, stories, music, and works of art that allow us to approach challenging topics indirectly, via metaphors. Instead of charging at life's biggest issues in a headlong, headstrong manner that silences that inner voice, we take Emily Dickinson's advice to "tell all the truth but tell it slant."[18]

By inviting people to explore hard questions in this way, we create conditions that allow the inner voice of truth to speak, the voice the physician heard. Those conditions are secured by some simple rules that help keep the space safe for the soul:

- Everything we offer during a retreat is an invitation, not an assignment, to which people may respond however they wish.
- We prohibit any attempts to fix, advise, save, or correct others, which frees people to speak and listen openly to one another.
- Instead of advising each other, we ask honest, open questions to help "hear people into deeper speech" and find their own inner answers.[19]
- We trust the silence, allowing it to underlie and infuse our dialogues.

- We maintain absolute confidentiality about things said during the retreat.[20]

In the space created by these rules, a conflicted physician was able to allow an essential truth to rise into full consciousness. The invitational nature of the space allowed him to sit silently for hours until he was ready to speak, all the while listening to others who were wrestling with similar dilemmas. The prohibition against advising allowed him to speak his truth knowing that he would be *heard,* not "fixed" with some facile comment. The group's trust in silence allowed him to speak his truth one hesitant step at a time until finally he was able to speak it to his most important audience: himself.

We need community to evoke the voice of the inner teacher. We need it as well to *test* what we believe the inner teacher is saying: not every voice we hear from within is the voice of truth. Testing does not mean other people telling us that we are right or wrong, which is less likely to lead to discernment than to fruitless arguments or mindless conformity. Testing, circle-of-trust-style, is a slow, patient process of speaking and listening without judgment—taking in what affirms us *and* what challenges us, together weaving a "tapestry of truth" that allows each person to sort out personal truth at his or her own depth and pace.

That is exactly what the troubled physician did as he listened to his peers explore their ethical dilemmas and reflected silently on his own in a space made safe for his healer's heart.

The Power of the Circle

Had it not been for the group he sat with, this physician might never have spoken his truth, even to himself. Clearly, he had heard inward whispers about the ethical cliff on which he was teetering, which is why he came burdened to the retreat. But when we keep recycling a hard truth inside our own heads, we easily get trapped in an endless loop.

Truth spoken silently to ourselves is not likely to take us anywhere: it is too easy to ignore it, defy it, or talk ourselves out of it.

However, when we are in a safe space—exploring our dilemmas with others and listening to them explore theirs—our internal conversations are freshened and sharpened and are more likely to become more truthful and more fruitful. When we speak our truth in community, it becomes harder to forget or deny that we said it and harder not to pursue its implications.

An ongoing circle of trust not only intensifies our sense of accountability to our own truth but also gives us a safe space in which to imagine and implement ways of witnessing to our integrity in the workplace. We can conduct small on-the-job experiments while we have access to a supportive community, returning to the circle to share our successes and failures with people who can help us learn from them. All of this increases the odds that the inner imperatives we touch will find expression in the outer world.

The physician who acknowledged that his Hippocratic Oath was at risk returned to his job and began to "speak the unspeakable" with one or two trusted colleagues. As he did, he discovered that he was not alone in his concerns at work any more than he was in the circle where he first spoke his truth. When we learn that we are surrounded by kindred souls, we begin to gather the imagination, courage, and collective power necessary to work for institutional transformation.

What does all this have to do with "healing the heart of democracy"? A great deal. The workplace where we spend so many hours of our lives is one of the prepolitical spaces where our habits of the heart get formed or deformed. It is a human-scale setting where questions arise about our capacity for mutual respect and trust, open listening and courageous speaking, and individual and collective resolve to work for the common good. The way we answer those questions in the workplace often spills over into the larger society, for better or for worse.

Suppose that more people in the financial services industry had confronted what was happening to their version of the Hippocratic Oath, their fiduciary responsibility to the people who invest in and purchase their products. Workplace citizenship of that sort might have reduced the number of Americans who lost their jobs and homes because too many people in financial services put self-service above service to others. Suppose that more public school teachers were to confront what is happening to their version of the Hippocratic Oath, the ethical responsibility they have to the children entrusted to their care. Workplace citizenship of that sort might energize an effective challenge to the distortions of high-stakes testing when it comes to serving the real needs of the young. Good citizenship is not limited to how we engage with the world of institutional politics. We play the citizen role at every level of our lives.

Helping people "nurture personal and professional integrity and the courage to act on it" in a community of peers is a vital step toward healing the heart of democracy. And yet circles of trust can take us only part of the way toward where the action is. These circles are halfway houses between those quiet, focused "monastic cells" where we can get the news from within and the noisy, crowded, rough-and-tumble spaces of the public and political worlds where democracy's heavy lifting gets done.

The physician who finally told himself the truth about his Hippocratic Oath was taken to the edge of political involvement, but he was not provided with direct access to it. Fortunately, there are spaces for deep democracy akin in spirit to circles of trust that open the political door wide and help people walk through it. History will show that what happens in such spaces can yield remarkable real-world results.

From Trust to Political Power

In the mid-1970s, I sat in a circle of rocking chairs at the Highlander Research and Education Center in Tennessee.[21] Twenty years earlier, this organization (then called the Highlander Folk School, founded in 1932 by a little-known hero of democracy named Myles Horton), had hosted a series of conversations between blacks and whites unprecedented in that time and place. Participants told personal stories; talked about social conditions; studied the theory, strategy, and tactics of nonviolent social change; and pondered and planned things that they might do to help bring a better world into being.

If rocking and talking seems far removed from the world of politics, consider this brief sketch of what happened as regional power brokers began to understand what the Highlander conversations had set in motion:

> In reaction to the effective work done by the school, during the late 1950s Southern newspapers attacked Highlander for supposedly creating racial strife. In 1957, the Georgia Commission on Education published a pamphlet titled "Highlander Folk School: Communist Training School in Monteagle, Tennessee." . . . Finally, in 1961, the state of Tennessee revoked Highlander's charter and confiscated its land and property.[22]

Those Tennessee politicians rightly perceived that the Highlander conversations had had radical implications. But the Georgia commissioners who attacked the school in print were wrong about the ideology that made Highlander "radical," a word whose original meaning suggests "reclaiming roots." The school was not creating communists: it was forming American citizens of the finest kind, rooted in democracy's first principles. The conversation partners at Highlander included Rosa Parks, Martin Luther King Jr., Ella Baker, Ralph Abernathy, Septima Clark, James Bevel, Bernard Lafayette, Bernice Robinson, and John Lewis. Together they planted the seeds of the Citizenship Schools,[23] the Montgomery bus boycott, the Student Nonviolent Coordinating Committee, and other key elements of the mid-twentieth-century civil rights movement.[24]

The moral of the Highlander story is simple: significant social change can come from people with a shared concern rocking and talking to each other—if they are willing to speak honestly and develop the skills to act competently on what they learn about themselves, each other, and the world. As the Highlander participants rocked and talked, they generated change of historic proportions, providing us with a model of personal exploration that goes beyond a circle of trust and merges seamlessly with political activism.

We need not go back half a century to prove the political power of this kind of notional space. A year or so before the 2008 presidential campaign went full throttle, I began to hear about "Camp Obama."[25] It captured my imagination in part because it created safe spaces for people to tell their own stories in ways that connected them with others who shared their social, economic, and political needs and interests. It struck me as a viable approach to making "We the People" a visible, palpable force.

But could Camp Obama produce results in the hardball world of practical politics? That is the question the journalist Zack Exley asked in a story he filed on August 29, 2007:

> No one who attends a "Camp Obama" training weekend can deny that something truly beautiful is taking place inside the Barack Obama campaign. But beauty does not win votes. Is the campaign's innovative, intellectual and emotional training program leading toward electoral power, or just another screaming disappointment for the grassroots? . . . There's no question that the leaders who attend gain a tremendous amount. There's no question that communities benefit from the leadership development that takes place at Camp Obama. . . . But is there time for this meticulous organization-building to make any kind of difference in the vote?[26]

Exley's question was answered decisively in the general election on November 4, 2008, when Barack Obama won the presidency "by a 6-point margin in the popular vote, 52 percent to 46 percent . . . [winning] more votes than any other individual in American history. Some 62,438,115 people cast their ballots for him."[27]

Obviously, Camp Obama was not the sole or most important reason for the Obama win, but it was a key ingredient. Regardless of ideology, political pragmatists have to admire what the process achieved. It mobilized hundreds of thousands of citizens, especially young people and people of color, who had effectively given up on American democracy and rarely, if ever, voted—and their votes pushed Obama over the top.

The Public Narrative Process

Camp Obama was designed by Marshall Ganz, a Harvard professor and community organizer. Organizing, as Ganz defines it, "combines the language of the heart as well as the head" because "it is values, not just interests" that move people to get involved in politics.[28] Ganz calls his process "public narrative," a values-based approach to organizing that breaks down some of the walls between us by appealing to our shared humanity.

Organizing based on shared values, says Ganz, "invites people to escape 'issue silos' and come together as complete human beings whose diversity is an asset to collective effort" instead of a barrier.[29] Values-based organizing

> allows us to communicate the values that motivate the choices that
> we make. Narrative is not talking "about" values; rather narrative
> embodies and communicates values. And it is through the shared
> experience of our values that we can engage with others, motivate one
> another to act, and find the courage to take risks, explore possibility,
> and face the challenges we must face.[30]

To frame his public narrative process, Ganz borrowed from an ancient spiritual tradition, adapting three famous questions posed by Rabbi Hillel the Elder two thousand years ago, questions I cited in Chapter VI: "If I am not for myself, who is for me? If I am only for myself, what am I? If not now, when?"[31] Participants in the process are briefed on the power of storytelling to move themselves and others into action. Then they are taught the basic elements of a well-constructed narrative—a plot, a protagonist, and a moral—and invited to craft and tell three stories under the rubrics suggested by Hillel's questions: the story of *self,* the story of *us,* and the story of *now.*[32]

As Ganz describes the nature of each of these stories, he touches on several of the key themes that run through this book:

> We all have a story of self. What's utterly unique about each of us is not the categories we belong to; what's utterly unique to us is our own journey of learning to be a full human being, a faithful person. And those journeys are never easy. They have their challenges, their obstacles, their crises. We learn to overcome them, and because of that we have lessons to teach. In a sense, all of us walk around with a text from which to teach, the text of our own lives.
>
> The second story is the story of us. That's an answer to the question, Why are we called? What experiences and values do we share as a community that call us to what we are called to? What is it about our experience of faith, public life, the pain of the world, and the hopefulness of the world? It's putting what we share into words. We've all been in places where people have worked together for years, but there's no *us* there because they don't share their stories. Faith traditions are grand stories of *us.* They teach how to be an *us.*
>
> Finally, there's the story of now—the fierce urgency of now. The story of now is realizing, after the sharing of values and aspirations, that the world out there is not as it ought to be. Instead, it is as it is. And that is a challenge to us. We need to appreciate the challenge and the conflict between the values by which we wish the world lived and the values by which it actually does. The difference between those two creates tension. It forces upon us consideration of a choice. What do we do about that? We're called to answer that question in a spirit of hope.
>
> Our goal is to meet this challenge, to seize this hope and turn it into concrete action. After developing our stories of self, then we work on building relationships, which forms the story of us. From there we turn to strategizing and action, working together to achieve a common purpose, learning to experience hope—that's the story of now.[33]

All of us live by the stories we tell about ourselves in the solitude of our own hearts, stories that help us make sense of our lives. Unfortunately, we have a tendency to tell stories that make the *self* powerless, *us* isolated, and the *now* hopeless. And yet something remarkable happens when we craft the kinds of stories that public narrative requires, stories that can be shared with other people. As we begin to understand that we are not alone in feeling powerless, isolated, and hopeless, we paradoxically begin to feel more powerful, united, and hopeful. As Ganz has written:

> A story communicates fear, hope, and anxiety, and because we can feel it, we get the moral not just as a concept, but as a teaching of our hearts. That's the power of story. That's why most of our faith traditions interpret themselves as stories, because they are teaching our hearts how to live as choiceful human beings capable of embracing hope over fear, self-worth and self-love over self-doubt, and love over isolation and alienation.[34]

In the public narrative process, stories are not therapeutic ends in themselves. They are ways to weave relationships that can empower political action of the sort the journalist Zack Exley describes:

> The story-telling exercises are the foundation of the model being used at Camp Obama. But they are not the end goal of the training. After a day of story telling, then came the nuts and bolts: training and exercises on how to function as an effective team, skills training for volunteer recruitment and voter contact, and review and explanations of field plans [for the districts in which the participants would soon be working].[35]

In the months, weeks, days, and hours leading up to November 4, 2008, people in cities across the country felt the ripple effects of Camp Obama. The three thousand volunteers who had been trained at the camp, along with thousands of others who had been trained by them, engaged hundreds of thousands of citizens in miniversions of the public narrative process, mobilizing millions of voters toward the goal of electing a Democratic president.[36]

All of this, of course, was fueled by political partisanship, which, rightly understood, is part of what makes democracy work. Can the Camp Obama process be uncoupled from partisan purposes and still retain its energy to achieve the larger goal of helping us reweave the tattered fabric of civic life? I am not certain that it can but I am certain that it must, if we want to reclaim a politics worthy of the human spirit.

Cyberspace and Deep Democracy

If I had been born in 1989 instead of 1939, cyberspace might have been the focus of this entire chapter. But my generation has come slowly and skeptically to the recognition that the Internet has become a public space—perhaps *the* public space—where people meet to share news and discuss issues as they once did at the crossroads or on the plaza.

Fifteen years ago, I was one of the skeptics. Today, I am one of millions who cannot imagine life without digital media. They allow me to stay in touch with family and friends, get news from a variety of sources, check and cross-check facts, do research related to my work, engage in dialogue with my readers, and collaborate with colleagues around the country to plan and implement projects and invite others into them.

In certain respects, cyberspace—"the notional environment in which communication over computer networks occurs"—has rendered physical space inefficient or obsolete.[37] Corporate executives in New York meet their Tokyo counterparts without leaving their offices. Merchants attract hordes of holiday shoppers who see nothing of each other except online consumer reviews of products. And thanks to Facebook, people have "friends" they have never met, most of whom understand the difference between Facebook "friends" and real friends.

Clearly, the Internet has major implications when it comes to the future of American democracy. The nature and magnitude of those implications is a much-disputed topic among close students of the digital revolution, two of whom are Clay Shirkey and Malcolm Gladwell. Shirkey's 2008 book *Here Comes Everybody: The Power of Organizing Without Organizations,* argues that the collaborations made possible by the World Wide Web are redistributing power, revolutionizing politics, and facilitating rapid social change.[38] Gladwell's 2010 *New Yorker* essay, "Small Change: Why the Revolution Will Not Be Tweeted," makes a counterargument.[39]

A *counterargument* is exactly what Gladwell makes. His essay begins with the story of the student sit-ins at the lunch counter of a downtown Woolworth's dime store in Greensboro, North Carolina. The first of these was on February 1, 1960. By the end of that month, Gladwell writes:

> There were sit-ins throughout the South, as far west as Texas. "I asked every student I met what the first day of the sitdowns had been like on his campus," the political theorist Michael Walzer wrote in *Dissent.* "The answer was always the same: 'It was like a fever. Everyone wanted to go.'" Some seventy thousand students eventually took part. Thousands were arrested and untold thousands more radicalized. These events in the early sixties became a civil-rights war that engulfed the South for the rest of the decade—and it happened without e-mail, texting, Facebook, or Twitter.[40]

Participation in these sit-ins spread fast and far because, according to Gladwell, the people involved had "strong ties" to one another. The ideas and feelings that animated their risky actions—and the courage needed to take them and keep taking them—leapt from friend to friend, multiplying geometrically. And that, says Gladwell, is what cannot happen in the "weak-tie" environment of Web-based social media:

> The kind of activism associated with social media isn't like this at all. The platforms of social media are built around weak ties. Twitter is a way of following (or being followed by) people you may never have

met. Facebook is a tool for efficiently managing your acquaintances, for keeping up with the people you would not otherwise be able to stay in touch with.[41]

In the weak-tie environment of cyberspace, information can spread farther and faster than it could in the 1960s. And yet, Gladwell argues, there is no substitute for the energy generated by a strong-tie environment when it comes to translating that information into social change.

Gladwell does us a service by challenging any facile notion that cyberspace is democracy's salvation—a challenge sharpened by Evgeny Morozov, who claims in his book, *The Net Delusion*, that cyberspace has benefited dictators more than dissidents.[42] However, a few months after Morozov's book was published, the journalist Roger Cohen documented the critical role Facebook played in the swift overthrow of a Tunisian dictator who had been firmly in power for nearly a quarter of a century.[43] And as this book heads into production, Egyptians are celebrating the overthrow of the thirty-year-old Mubarak regime, the result of a popular uprising aided and abetted in significant measure by Facebook and Twitter.

Clearly, the Internet is yet another tool whose value depends on how it is used. So there is no need to pit these analysts against each other—all have pieces of the puzzle when it comes to understanding the Internet's role in politics. The lunch counter sit-ins, like other nonviolent actions across the South in the 1960s, certainly required strong ties. But those ties might have been strengthened even further by the rapid spread of information via digital media.[44] Conversely, the strong ties created by Marshall Ganz's public narrative process would not have had the political impact they did without the Obama campaign's sophisticated use of weak-tie technology.[45]

The question of how the digital media might affect democracy becomes more interesting to me when we ask what happens to our habits of the heart when we "meet" in cyberspace. Here is a brief flashback to the five key habits of the heart named in Chapter II, followed by some of the pluses and minuses I see as we move deeper into the era of digital connectedness:

- An understanding that we are all in this together
- An appreciation of the value of "otherness"
- The ability to hold tension in life-giving ways
- A sense of personal voice and agency
- A greater capacity to create community

Because the Internet allows us to connect with people at great geographic and experiential remove, we have a chance to expand and deepen our sense of sharing a common life. In the process of writing this book, I have had digital dialogues with Americans of many stripes, as well as people from half a dozen other nations. All of them share my concerns about democracy, and some of them share my convictions. More than a few of these exchanges resulted in midcourse corrections of my writing—and as a rule, I have found them both edifying and cordial.

The relatively rare exceptions to that rule occurred only when my "conversation partner" was anonymous, believed that I was dead wrong, and instead of debating the issue, impugned my intelligence or my character. It might be argued that in those moments I had a chance to exercise my ability to hold tension creatively. I confess that that is not what happened; instead, I simply logged off. It is hard to take seriously the opinions of a masked ranter who screeches a drive-by curse and speeds off before you can respond. Some tensions are not worth holding.

Still, the Internet has given me other opportunities to learn to hold tension creatively. While writing this book, I spent hundreds of hours checking out what I thought were facts only to find that they were not and testing my opinions against the views of commentators I had come to respect though they differ from me politically. The fact that I could do this slowly and reflectively—as long as I avoided the temptation to break the tension by clicking on every link in sight—allowed me to entertain diverse viewpoints in a way that has enriched my thinking and, I hope, this book.

The Web has also helped me find more of my voice on things I care about and deepen my sense of agency as I watched consequences flow from my words in the form of new conversations, gatherings, projects, and programs. Of course, those consequences came not merely because I spoke. They came because others joined their voices to mine, including people who might not have spoken had we been face-to-face. To borrow a phrase from Garrison Keillor of *Prairie Home Companion* fame, the Internet "gives shy people the strength to get up and do what needs to be done." Cyberspace can facilitate the kinds of connections that get people working together, people who would never have met had it not been for this "notional space."

As I have seen how cyberspace can help us form democratic habits of the heart, I have also seen how it can deform us. The more we live in virtual communities, the more privatized our lives become, undermining the foundations of our public and political life. Buying a book online with the click of a mouse and receiving it at home two days later (or instantly as a digital download) is more convenient than patronizing a local bookstore. But every time we choose convenience over human contact, our sense of being part of a civic community is dulled. Spend enough time buying books online, and we will forget that a bookstore's purpose is not merely to sell books but to provide a place where the company of strangers can gather—to say nothing of the fact that we may well lose our local independent or chain bookstore.

The Internet also threatens democracy by making it easier for falsehoods related to politics to gain credence and multiply, giving aid and comfort to the enemies of common sense, decency, and truth. It is good for democracy that the digital media allow more and more of us to become producers as well as consumers of political opinions and information. It is not good when, as consumers, we make no effort to question what we read, compare it to other sources, and attempt to separate the wheat from the chaff. Some of the new producers are among our finest journalists, while others are apparently devoted to making Orwellian prophecies come true. As consumers of their wares, we need to set our bunk detectors on high.

Democracy is also endangered by the fact that cyberspace tends to attract people of similar socioeconomic status. I am far from the first to worry about the "digital divide," the gulf between those who have easy access to technology and the resources and skills to use it. That divide makes it difficult to meet up with genuine otherness in cyberspace, a difficulty that mirrors our longtime and deepening social-class divide. But because the digital media hold great promise for facilitating encounters across such lines, bridging the digital divide is a key to democracy's future.

Meeting that challenge demands more of us than time, money, and well-designed educational programs. It demands that we transcend our fears and embrace dialogue with the "alien other" for the value it can add to our lives. We are a tribal species, and dealing with otherness is difficult for most of us no matter where we encounter it. In the midst of a contentious online dialogue between apparently irreconcilable viewpoints, I have sometimes found myself tempted to leave the room—even though I would not think of walking out if we were in a face-to-face debate.

When a situation like that arises, I try to remember the Manhattan taxi driver I wrote about in Chapter V, whose passion for dialogue in the company of strangers trumps the fact that, in his words, "you never know who's getting into the cab, so it's a little dangerous." The sporadic dangers he faced in his taxi are several orders of magnitude greater than those I face in cyberspace, which have nothing to do with my physical safety and everything to do with my ego.

That cabbie loved the "blooming, buzzing confusion" of democracy despite its occasional risks. I doubt that he is still with us. But if he were, I feel certain of two things: he would want to continue to mix and mingle with flesh-and-blood people in three-dimensional space *and* he would love cyberspace, which blooms and buzzes with confusion and vitality in a way that would delight his heart.

CHAPTER VIII

The Unwritten History
of the Heart

For there is a boundary to looking.
And the world that is looked at so deeply
wants to flourish in love.

Work of the eyes is done, now
go and do heart-work

on all the images imprisoned within you.

—RAINER MARIA RILKE, "Turning Point"[1]

When you die, someone will write your obituary. It will tell readers when and where you were born and what kind of work you did. It may name where you went to school and celebrate some of your achievements and personal qualities. It will identify those who survive you and perhaps say something about what you meant to them.

And yet even the longest, most detailed, and most expressive obituaries always omit the essence of a life: the history of a person's heart. How many of us wish that we had asked more questions of someone we loved, not about what happened and when but about the inner experience of being that person? About hopes and fulfillments, failures and regrets? About moments of despair and moments of meaning? Even as that wish moves through us, we know it is well-nigh impossible for a person to tell us the history of his or her heart. After all, we can barely articulate our own.

The heart of the world itself has an unwritten history. Historians write about visible movements: the movements of populations, cultural artifacts, and technologies; natural resources and money; armed forces and political power. But as the poet Rilke reminds us, "there is a boundary to looking." The deeper movements that shape our world are impulses of the heart invisible to the eye: the hopes and greeds that move markets; the loves and hates that rouse armies; the desires to create or control that galvanize political power.

In this book, I have tried to look at visible political realities without losing sight of the heart that animates them. As the book comes to a close, I want to say a few words about the unwritten history of the heart in the world of politics. I will do it by taking a clue from the poet Rilke, tracking what happens when we "go and do heart-work / on all the images imprisoned within" us.

This is the inner work that all successful movements for social change have done, not least the movement called American democracy. They have done it in spite of the challenges of unearthing and telling the heart's story—challenges that become especially daunting when the story to be told is one that powerful forces in the world do not want to hear.

Myth and the Story of the Heart

What does it mean to do "heart-work" on our imprisoned inner images? One approach is to name, claim, and examine the myths that animate our personal or collective lives, myths that give voice to deep movements of the heart. *Myth* is a tricky word. People often interpret it as meaning an outright lie ("We kids were told that Dad was stationed overseas when in fact he was in prison") or a sincere but untrue belief when it is taken literally ("God created the world in six days"). Rightly understood, a myth is an effort to tell truths that cannot be told with mere facts or known by the senses and the mind alone, truths that take form only in that integrative place called the heart.

In 1930, a Sioux medicine man named Black Elk dictated the tragic story of his people to a white writer named John G. Neihardt. Black Elk began by telling Neihardt the Sioux myth of the sacred pipe and how "the pipe first came to us." After narrating this tale—which sounds fantastical to people who rely exclusively on facts that can be seen by looking—Black Elk said, "Whether it happened so I do not know; but if you think about it, you can see that it is true."[2] Of course, the Sioux are not alone in having stories that might be described this way. Adherents of every religious tradition have them, as witness their various creation stories. And citizens of every nation have them, including Americans, as in the notion that our nation has a special status and destiny in the eyes of God.

If we want to learn something about the history of the heart, there is one more thing we need to know about the nature of myths. Myths do more than name truths that lie deeper than mere facts, truths that will never show up in data that historians would find credible. They also name aspirations that *might* be achieved in the facts of our lives but remain as yet unfulfilled—possibilities that, in the wry words of the historian Daniel J. Boorstein, "have not yet gone through the formality of taking place."[3]

When we openly acknowledge this gap between aspiration and reality and are willing to live in it honestly, a myth can encourage us to bring what we *are* a bit closer to what we *seek to be*. When we confuse the aspiration with the reality of our lives, we can get ourselves into very deep trouble as individuals and as a nation. The example closest at hand is one that I know well.

My early life was shaped by a "golden boy" myth of myself, a fact I did not understand until my early adulthood. The myth was seeded in me long before I achieved adult consciousness and was nurtured by good fortune and dumb luck into my late teens. My life flowed along quite pleasantly—until the reality of who I was began to collide with my buried myth. Slowly I started to realize that I was not the golden boy that my myth made me out to be. Filled with a sense of failure and loss, my golden boy glow replaced by the heat of shame and guilt, I found myself consumed by anger and then by heartbreak.

My effort to understand that heartbreak drove me to do what Rilke calls heart-work. First I needed to see that my unconscious self-image had caused ego inflation, creating a personal reality that was self-centered and self-obsessed. A golden boy makes no mistakes and has no reason to believe "lesser beings" when they claim that he has—and that, of course, is a big mistake. Then I needed to understand that I could not become whole until I acknowledged the myth that I had been living by, grieved the gap between it and the reality of my life, and set out on the long journey to integrate my liabilities with my gifts, my darkness with my light.

Integrate is the key word here. Having raised my myth to awareness, where I could work free of its unconscious grip, I did not need to destroy it. Alongside the big lie it told me, my golden boy myth contained some achievable aspirations that I needed to hold on to; for example, the simple desire to do good work and to be good to others. I do have *some* gold in me, along with my share of dross. Integration means being able to say to myself, "I am both my shadow and my light, and the two cannot be separated."

As I began to integrate the two sides of myself—the two sides of everything human—my awareness of the dross helped keep me grounded, and my awareness of the gold called me toward my best self, reminding me of the "better angels of my nature."

America's National Myths

Nations, like individuals, have myths rooted deep in their histories, myths that are always contradicted by their complex realities. Americans do not need to dig deep to find some of this country's key myths: they are headlined and highlighted in the documents that created this nation.

Among the nation's founders were men who had profound insight into the human condition as well as a profound command of the English language. By doing what could fairly be called heart-work, they gave powerful and poetic voice to those "images imprisoned within" the millions who sought freedom from Old World cruelties and constraints. As they raised those imprisoned images to consciousness, they also raised an army, loosing powers that made world history.

These men penned what the historian Joseph Ellis calls "the most potent and consequential words in American history, perhaps in modern history," the words that comprise the first few lines of the Declaration of Independence.[4] Many of us know these lines by heart, not merely because of repetition but because the yearning behind them remains deep in our hearts to this day:

> We hold these truths to be self-evident, that all men are created equal,
> that they are endowed by their Creator with certain unalienable
> Rights, that among these are Life, Liberty and the pursuit of Happi-
> ness. That to secure these rights, Governments are instituted among
> Men, deriving their just powers from the consent of the governed.

Thus was created an American myth—perhaps *the* American myth—in two senses of the word. On the one hand, the people who wrote those words, and the nation they founded, fell far short of their own declaration. The founders excluded many men and all women from the "blessings of liberty," and in this sense, America's founding myth is a flat-out lie. On the other hand, the myth expresses an aspiration without which America would not be the nation it is. Our desire to be a nation that honors human equality has proved so powerful that we have been compelled to pursue it for nearly two and a half centuries, a task that will continue to occupy us as long as this nation exists.

If we remain clear about the gap between America's aspiration and its reality, our founding myth can continue to energize movement toward our goal. But when we imagine or pretend that it describes

America's reality, the myth becomes an enemy of its own aspiration. Then, for example, when we see clear evidence of radical inequality in our midst—such as who has the best chance of getting a good education or holding wealth or living a long and healthy life or ending up in jail—we explain it away by qualifying our myth: "All people are created equal *if* they are willing to make the effort to be equal." Now our mythical self-image gives us protective cover for holding the oppressed responsible for the sins of the oppressors. Now we relieve ourselves of the responsibility to close the gap between our vision of possibility and the reality of our common life.

The fact that America's national myth is so easily accessed in words of poetic power is a curse as well as a blessing. It took me several years of inner work to unearth my own buried golden boy self-image and get an accurate account of the history of my own heart. Americans are blessed by the fact that we can unearth key elements of our national image in a New York minute: all we need do to remind ourselves of who we want to be is recite a few words from the Declaration, the Constitution, the Pledge of Allegiance, or our national anthem. At the same time, we are cursed by the fact that our facile command of our myth makes it easy for us to believe that it names our reality as a nation—and equally easy to accuse anyone who questions it of being unpatriotic or worse.

As a nation, we are not compelled to do what I and many others have to do on our continuing journey toward personal wholeness: dig down day by day through the rubble of our mistakes and malfeasances to recover our buried self-images—a process that forces us to compare them to reality, host an ongoing dialogue between the better and lesser angels of our nature, and develop at least a modicum of humility. All we Americans need to do is chant "one nation under God, indivisible, with liberty and justice for all," and we get a booster shot of national and delusional self-righteousness.

At our national worst, we have chutzpah without humility. We will retain this adolescent trait as long as we are unwilling to confront the gap between who we are and who we want to be—a process that will always take us through a place called humiliation.

When Image and Reality Collide

Today, America is going through a collective version of the collision I experienced in my own life, but much of it is happening unconsciously. Our national myths are contradicted by certain realities about who we are, and yet we continue to maintain the pretense that our myths describe reality: in a December 2010 poll, 80 percent of us called the United States "the greatest country in the world."[5]

Amid the turmoil of what some have called the "politics of rage," I have been reminded of the anger I felt as my own golden boy myth began to be revealed as the lie that it was. I have also been reminded of my discovery that behind my anger was deep grief over the fact that I was not nearly as noble as I had imagined myself to be. That parallel is what led me to see that the politics of rage is more aptly named the "politics of the brokenhearted."

When we begin to see that our myths do not square with the reality we are living—but we have yet to face the contradiction squarely—the result is an upheaval of denial and dysfunction that, left unchecked, can bring us down. Some of America's political pathologies result from the fact that we keep trying desperately to save face, just as I did when I began to realize that I was not pure gold.

For example, as recently as 2007, some 41 percent of Americans agreed with the statement that Iraq was "directly involved in planning, financing, or carrying out" the terrorist attacks of September 11, 2001.[6] Why do so many people believe a proposition that has been proved false so decisively? The answer goes much deeper than the fact that an oft-repeated lie can take on the appearance of truth.

Many Americans are caught up in the collective version of my unconscious personal conviction that "it is impossible for a golden boy to do wrong" and that it is impermissible for others to claim that he has. As long as we continue to delude ourselves this way, the gap between myth and reality will continue to cause upheaval. As individuals and as a nation, there is an intimate connection between our capacity to "get real" and our capacity to get well.

Over the years, our national golden boy myth has taken different forms. All of them are laced with lies, and all of them will continue to sicken us—until we get well enough to reclaim the legitimate aspirations they contain. Here are some of the versions of that myth we are living with today:

• *America is the world's leading superpower.* If this means that the United States is the global leader in military spending, it is not a lie. It is a simple statement of fact.[7] But if it describes our ability to achieve major foreign policy goals by means of military might, then a lie it is, at least in large part. Not since World War II has our superpower self-image squared with the reality of what we have been able to accomplish internationally via war or the threat of war.

• *The American economy is capable of endless growth.* The rate of economic growth we have known since World War II cannot be sustained, and the Great Recession from which we may now be emerging is a harbinger of that fact. Many factors play into this "new reality"—a reality that some prophets have been warning us about for a very long time, especially those who have pointed to the rapid rate at which we have been depleting the earth's nonrenewable resources.

• *America offers more economic opportunity than any nation on earth.* The fact is that we are currently in seventh or eighth place in opportunities for upward mobility, behind several Scandinavian and European nations. We can no longer promise our children a standard of living superior to that of our generation, unless they want to emigrate.[8] For immigrants from countries that are worse off than America and its peers, there are good reasons to come here, but joining the rapidly vanishing middle class is not likely to be one of them. Still, the lie persists: in 2008, some 40 percent of Americans with incomes under $20,000 a year identified themselves as middle class.[9]

• *America is a "melting pot" where everyone wants to "be an American."* This myth of assimilation—that everyone speaks the same language, aspires to identical goals, and seeks to live similar lifestyles—must now give way to the fact that many immigrants who want to be Americans also want to retain their own language and culture. As Supreme Court Justice Sonia Sotomayor put it in a 2001 speech, we live in the "tension between 'the melting pot and the salad bowl'—a recently popular metaphor used to describe New York's diversity."[10]

Taken together, myths like these have been foundations of national pride, and we have taken their truth for granted. The rumbles we feel in the land are not merely those caused by ideological clashes and the so-called politics of rage. The deeper rumbles are caused by the cracking of our foundations, the visible failures of our invisible national mythology.

If we want to reclaim our democracy, we need to do the challenging heart-work of examining our myths, seeing how far they are from the reality of our national life, then reclaiming their embedded visions and doing the hard work necessary to bring reality closer to them.

Embedded in the superpower myth is a vision of global stability, which depends in part on a few nations having enough power and consensus on issues of peace and justice to protect minority rights and keep outlaw nations in line. We can realize this aspiration only by developing genuinely collaborative relationships with our potential partners, a development that requires more humility than chutzpah.

Embedded in America's mythology of endless economic growth and opportunity is the dream of a society that is not deeply divided between the rich and the poor, a society with a healthy middle class that is truly open to all. This dream is dying fast in our land. It can be revived only by radically rethinking our economic assumptions and altering our personal and collective approaches to consumption.

Embedded in the melting pot myth is a vision America has named as "*E pluribus unum,*" the notion that out of human diversity can come one people. This aspiration does not mean suppressing diversity. It means transcending the fear that leads to suppression so that we can celebrate the creative potentials inherent in the "many" who come together as "one," honoring uniqueness as well as commonality.

Movements and the History of the Heart

In practical political terms, what does it mean to reclaim the aspirations found in our myths and work toward achieving them? The best answer to that question is found by studying the great movements for social change—movements that have made a difference in the lay and the law of the land, movements so well chronicled that they provide the closest thing we have to a *written* history of the heart of politics.

Look, for example, at the international movement for women's rights; the movements for liberation in South Africa, eastern Europe, and Latin America; the American civil rights movement of the twentieth century; and the never-ending movement called American democracy that began in 1776. The history of these momentous processes of change points to a simple fact: without an uprising of vision and energy among those who suffer most from the gap between vision and reality, little progress can be made on the challenges facing humankind.

Movements of social transformation are sparked by people who are isolated, marginalized, and oppressed but who do not fall into despair. Instead, they respond to their condition by taking the poet Rilke's advice that we go inward "and do heart-work / on all the images imprisoned within" us. Having released those images, they return to the world of action resolved to live in a way that will help it become a place in which their humanity is honored. Under the right conditions, their witness can tap a collective yearning that contains enough energy to move the world closer to the heart's aspirations.

The first stage of all social movements lies in what I have called the "Rosa Parks decision." Rosa Parks did not launch the American civil rights movement by herself, to say the obvious. She became the public icon of a long line of oppressed African Americans who had an "imprisoned image" of themselves as free women and men while being externally imprisoned by cultural and institutional racism. Rosa Parks spoke for all of them when she made the decision to "live divided no more," to act outwardly in a way that reflected the truth she knew inwardly: that she was nothing less than a human being, whole and worthy and free.[11]

On December 1, 1955, in Montgomery, Alabama, when Rosa Parks refused to yield her seat on the bus to a white man, sparking a movement was not at the front of her mind. As Parks famously said, she kept her seat on that bus because she was tired—not in her body but in her soul—tired of consenting to being treated as "less." Of course, she acted in the context of a community, of a shared social concern, and of a theory of nonviolent social change. Among other things, Parks served as secretary of the Montgomery chapter of the National Association for the Advancement of Colored People (NAACP) and had participated in sessions at the Highlander Folk School on the tactics and strategies of nonviolence.[12] And yet in the moment a person acts on the decision to live an undivided life, strategic considerations take a distant second to the power of the heart's demands.

That decision is often made at personal risk—the risk of losing your reputation, your friends, your livelihood, and sometimes even your life. We cannot find the courage to take such risks by calculating the odds that our actions will trigger something big. There is no guarantee that anyone will stand with us or that what we do will release larger energies.

We have only one guarantee: the knowledge that by living divided no more, we are claiming our own identity and integrity in the midst of a hostile world. As more than a few people can attest, that fact is compensation enough for whatever punishment may follow. As Rosa Parks said to the police who threatened to put her in jail if she refused to yield her seat, "You may do that." What a remarkable way of saying, "What could your jail of stone and steel possibly mean to me? By acting on the images of true self that were imprisoned in my own heart, I have just freed myself from a jail far worse than yours."

Rosa Parks and others like her—such as South Africa's Nelson Mandela, Myanmar's Aung San Suu Kyi, Czechoslovakia's Václav Havel, and some of America's founders—found the courage to take profound personal risks by transforming their notion of punishment. All of them came to understand that *no punishment anyone might lay on us could possibly be greater than the punishment we lay on ourselves by conspiring in our own diminishment.* The decision to live divided no more is a decision to end that conspiracy by bringing one's life into congruence with the imperatives of the heart.

Obviously, no social movement can be sustained by isolated individual decisions to witness to personal truth, no matter how many people are involved. So movements for social change—which begin with the deeply inward decision to live "divided no more"—must gain adherents, energy, organization, savvy, and traction by evolving through three more stages of development that take them into the outer world with transformative power.*

From Inner Liberation to Outer Transformation

Stage two involves the formation of "communities of congruence," such as that tiny independent black church near Americus, Georgia (Chapter II), or the Highlander Folk School, or a circle of trust (Chapter VII). In communities like these, people gather to support each other's resolve to live by the heart's imperatives.

The inner decision that sparks social movements is not easy to sustain in a culture that commends the divided life as the safe and sane way to go. People who make the "Rosa Parks decision" can easily become discouraged as they try to explain themselves to uncomprehending family and friends, losing time, energy, and even their resolve in the process. They need kindred spirits to reassure themselves that they are not crazy, and reassurance is one of the things a community of congruence provides.

---

*Because the heart is the home of everything human, the darkness as well as the light, the movements that emerge from it include some that are democratic and some that are authoritarian. My "stage theory" of the way movements unfold applies to both types, as a theory should, although the two often diverge in stage three: democratic movements "go public" while authoritarian movements do not. All of my illustrations here, however, are of the democratic type.

People who are on this path also need the dispositions, knowledge, and skills that will allow them to enter the political fray and make their voices heard. So communities of congruence help people develop the habits of the heart that agents of social change, and all engaged citizens, must possess. They help people master the information, theories, and strategies that will allow them to advance their cause. And they offer people small-scale opportunities to become the kinds of leaders that a large-scale movement demands.

Communities of congruence are like nurseries or hothouses where plants are tended until they are hearty enough to be transplanted outdoors and subjected to all kinds of weather. In a circle of trust, for example, participants are able to speak the vulnerable language of the heart in the presence of people who affirm it instead of tearing it down, as in the case of the physician who acknowledged that his Hippocratic Oath was at risk (Chapter VII). As participants continue to make themselves vulnerable in a nurturing environment, the heart's language grows more robust and slowly becomes their "new normal." Eventually, the day comes when they find themselves speaking their hearts in public, having almost forgotten that doing so once seemed impossibly risky.

In this way—and in other, more intentional and strategic ways—a movement segues into stage three, which involves "going public." The importance of this stage seems simple and self-evident. If a movement did not go public in order to spread its message and try to create social change, it would be a secret society, not a movement. But there is another, equally important reason why a movement must go public if it is to become a force for good: only by doing so can a movement gain the critics it needs.

The shadow side of any movement is the belief that "we are right and everyone else is wrong," a belief that goes unchallenged when people talk only with those who share their views. When movement advocates fail to go public where they attract and must engage the critics, their self-protective closed loop creates a collective narcissism, one of the pathologies at the heart of fascism and its kin. True believers in the movement become insufferable, and the movement starts inflicting suffering on its opponents, defaming rather than engaging anyone who sees things differently. At the extremes, this results in the fascist "solution" of jailing or killing the movement's critics.

A movement can be saved from these antidemocratic consequences only by openly engaging those who disagree. If the critics are wrong, the movement can answer them in public, gaining a chance to advance its case in the court of public opinion even if the critics are not convinced. And if the critics are right, the movement has a chance to correct itself before its own limitations and errors bring it down. A legitimate movement works hard to keep its critics in the conversation, and there is no better example of this than the movement called American democracy.

In the fourth stage of a movement, signs of success appear. I am not referring to the "big wins" that make headline news, such as the passage of the Civil Rights Act of 1964, the Velvet Revolution that freed Czechoslovakia in 1989, or the election of Nelson Mandela as president of South Africa in 1994. Successes such as these were the result of a million invisible acts of courage and the incremental gains that came with them, the micro-moments in which the history of the heart is written.

A movement's success is signaled by a slow accretion of small changes in the system of institutional rewards and punishments by which all societies exercise social control. Qualities, commitments, and actions for which people in an earlier era were unjustly punished begin to become sources of reward in a process so gradual that it attracts little notice. For example, as the civil rights movement gained momentum, a few educators and scholars saw a new day coming, one that required them to rethink the way they did their work. American history had to be revisited and rewritten from the standpoint of an oppressed minority. If students were to thrive in a multicultural world, they would need to understand it. And if these needs were to be met, our educational institutions needed more people of color as students, teachers, and scholars.

As a result of this awakening, actions that would have led to retributions in prior decades began leading to careers and even prestige in the field of education. These and similar small, incremental changes in other fields preceded the passage of the Civil Rights Act of 1964. Cumulatively, they helped create the political momentum that compelled Congress to put the force of law behind a transformed system of rewards and punishments, giving oppressed groups legal protection against discrimination.

In this fourth stage of a movement, there is an inward as well as an outward transformation, and it brings us back full circle to stage one. A movement gets under way as advocates realize that no punishment could possibly be greater than the one we lay on ourselves by conspiring in our own diminishment. In the final phase of a movement, advocates begin to understand that no *reward* could possibly be greater than the one we give ourselves by living our own truth "out loud" and in the light of day.

I cannot imagine a spiritual pain deeper than dying with the thought that during my sojourn on earth, I had rarely, if ever, shown up as my true self. And I cannot imagine a spiritual comfort deeper than dying with the knowledge that I had spent my brief time on this planet doing the best I could to be present as myself to my family, my friends, my community, and my world.

Standing and Acting with Hope in the Tragic Gap

These four stages—deciding to live "divided no more," forming communities of congruence, going public with a vision, and transforming the system of punishment and reward—are found in every social movement I have studied. Of course, history is messier than the movement model suggests. These stages do not come with clear beginnings and endings. Nor do they follow on one another like parts moving down an assembly line, emerging as a product called social change. Instead, they intertwine in a process that looks like the double-helix strands of a DNA molecule generating organic life.

As long as we do not confuse this model with how things happen in the real world, extracting stages from the complexity of life serves two important purposes. It gives us X-ray vision to see how movements unfold amid the chaos of history, observing inner and outer dynamics we might otherwise miss. And once we have seen what animates a movement we care about, we have a better sense of where that movement is in its development—and what we must do to keep it moving along.

The organic renewal generated by a movement eventually withers and dies, setting the stage for yet another movement. The movement called American democracy is no exception. In every generation, we must try again to close the gap between our reality and our aspirations. That gap will always be open, and the hearts of those who try to close it will always be broken. As I come to the end of this book, a tragic example is close at hand.

In Chapter II, I said that my first experience of political heartbreak came in 1963 with the assassination of John F. Kennedy. Now, as I write this paragraph, my heart has been broken again, as have millions of others. It is Saturday, January 8, 2011, nearly fifty years since Kennedy was killed. This morning, outside a supermarket in Tucson, Arizona, a gunman killed six people and wounded fourteen others at a "Congress on Your Corner" event sponsored by United States Representative Gabrielle Giffords of Arizona's Eighth District.

Congresswoman Giffords was gravely wounded. The dead include U.S. District Judge John McCarthy Roll and nine-year-old Christina Taylor Green. Christina—a third-grader who had just been elected to her school's student council and came to the event to learn more about democracy—was well on her way at a very young age to becoming an engaged citizen.

The gunman is almost certainly mentally ill, and for some Americans, that is the end of the story. Others argue that the accusatory, inflammatory, and sometimes violent rhetoric of our political life contributed to his murderous act. I do not know whether that is true, and I doubt that anyone ever will: how do you get inside a profoundly deranged mind? But I do know this: violence comes in many forms, from spiritual to physical, and every form is rooted in a failure of compassion, a lack of empathy and respect.

There may be no direct causal link between a psychopathic act and a political climate of vitriol, contempt, and lies. And yet all of this and more can be found along a continuum of heartless uncaring. The deranged individual has an excuse that the rest of us lack: his or her brain is wired in a way that makes empathy impossible. For the rest of us, caring or not caring for each other is a choice we make in political as well as personal life. Ultimately, it is a choice between death and life.

For fifty years, I have walked with and learned from people who witness against violence in its many forms. For the last six of those years, I have worked on this book, making a case for a nonviolent politics in which creative conflict is possible. During the past half-century, I have often seen our "better angels" at work, sometimes against great odds. I have also seen their shadowy counterparts drive us to violence time and time again, breaking my heart and challenging me to hold the tension between the light and the dark.

Of all the tensions we must hold in personal and political life, perhaps the most fundamental and most challenging is standing and acting with hope in the "tragic gap." On one side of that gap, we see the hard realities of the world, realities that can crush our spirits and defeat our hopes. On the other side of that gap, we see real-world possibilities, life as we know it *could* be because we have seen it that way. We see a world at war, but we have known moments of peace. We see racial and religious enmity, but we have known moments of unity. We see suffering caused by unjust scarcities, but we have known moments of material and spiritual sharing in which abundance was generated. Possibilities of this sort are not wishful dreams or fantasies: they are alternative realities that we have witnessed in our own lives.

Nonetheless, we continue to live our lives in the tragic gap—tragic not simply because it is heartbreaking but because, in the classical sense of *tragic,* it is an eternal and inescapable feature of the human condition. This is the place called human history where we must stand and act with hope even though neither we nor any of our descendants will see the gap permanently closed.

As we stand in this hard place, it is difficult to imagine staying there for the long haul. Our constant temptation is to allow the tension between reality and possibility to pull us one way or the other. If we are pulled toward too much reality, we fall into corrosive cynicism. Having seen "how the world works," as with its recurrent violence, we arm ourselves and prepare for war rather than work for peace, thus becoming part of the problem. If we are pulled toward too much possibility, we fall into irrelevant idealism. Then we live in the fantasy world of "Wouldn't it be nice if . . . ," floating so far above the fray that we lose our grip on what *is,* becoming part of the problem in yet another way. Cynicism and idealism sound like opposites, and yet they have the same result: both take us out of the action by pulling us out of the tragic gap.

America's founders realized that generation after generation of citizens would need to stay *in* the action lest the political movement they planted wither and die. So they built opportunities for continual renewal into democracy's infrastructure. Though they did not speak of the "tragic gap," they clearly embraced the essence of the idea. As the journalist Jon Meachum observed in his review of Joseph Ellis's *American Creation:*

> How to live in a tragic milieu and yet strive toward triumph—for while perfection may not be possible, progress is—was a consuming concern for the founders, who, led by James Madison, made a virtue of creating competing centers of power within the constitutional structure. . . . To transform disagreement from a natural source of strife into a source of stability was a crucial insight, and is arguably the great achievement of the Constitution. What frustrates the passionate about America—its creaky checks and balances, diffuse sovereignties and general aversion to sudden change—is, Ellis argues, what makes possible the triumphs we do manage to pull off.[13]

If we are to stand and act with hope in the tragic gap and do it for the long haul, we cannot settle for mere "effectiveness" as the ultimate measure of our failure or success. Yes, we want to be effective in pursuit of important goals. But when measurable, short-term outcomes become the only or primary standard for assessing our efforts, the upshot is as pathetic as it is predictable: we take on smaller and smaller tasks—the only kind that yield instantly visible results—and abandon the large, impossible but vital jobs we are here to do.

We must judge ourselves by a higher standard than effectiveness, the standard called faithfulness. Are we faithful to the community on which we depend, to doing what we can in response to its pressing needs? Are we faithful to the better angels of our nature and to what they call forth from us? Are we faithful to the eternal conversation of the human race, to speaking and listening in a way that takes us closer to truth? Are we faithful to the call of courage that summons us to witness to the common good, even against great odds? When faithfulness is our standard, we are more likely to sustain our engagement with tasks that will never end: doing justice, loving mercy, and calling the beloved community into being.

Full engagement in the movement called democracy requires no less of us than full engagement in the living of our own lives. We carry the past with us, so we must understand its legacy of deep darkness as well as strong light. We can see the future only in imagination, so we must continue to dream of freedom, peace, and justice for everyone. Meanwhile, we live in the present moment, with its tedium and terror, its fears and hopes, its incomprehensible losses and its transcendent joys. It is a moment in which it often feels as if nothing we do will make a difference, and yet so much depends on us.

The theologian Reinhold Niebuhr understood all of this deeply and well. He wrote the best words I know to bring this book to a close:

> Nothing that is worth doing can be achieved in our lifetime; there-fore, we must be saved by hope. Nothing which is true or beautiful or good makes complete sense in any immediate context of history; therefore, we must be saved by faith. Nothing we do, however virtu-ous, can be accomplished alone; therefore we are saved by love.[14]

[GRATITUDES]

This book, my ninth, has been the most challenging. When I first felt called to write it, I tried to hang up the phone. I knew the topic was important, but I also knew that exploring it would mean negotiating some hazardous terrain. I felt too old, weary, and disheartened to take the job on, let alone to do it well.

I cannot claim to have found the fountain of youth. But writing the book has rejuvenated me, perhaps because I survived it! Nor can I claim to have done the job well. That, of course, is for others to judge. What I can say is that I now feel better equipped to engage creatively in the conflicts of democracy as a citizen who cares about the common good.

I would not have been able to start or finish this book without the love, encouragement, and practical assistance of a number of people. I owe all of them my deepest gratitude.

Sheryl Fullerton, my longtime editor at Jossey-Bass, believes in me as a writer and understands what I hope to accomplish with my writing. This time around, when I had lost faith in myself, she helped me believe I could write another book but never shied away from pressing me to get it right. I am lucky to have her as a good friend as well as a good colleague.

Sharon Palmer, my wife, supports me in all those ways and so many more, and she does it day in and day out, for which I am endlessly grateful. She is also my first-line editor, a thoughtful and tireless reader who is relentless when she thinks I have it wrong and cries when I get it right: I kid you not! She asks three questions as she reads: Is it worth saying? Is it said clearly? Is it said beautifully? Much of this book falls short of her three-part test. But because of her faith and love, both the book and its author are better by far than they would otherwise be.

Christine Craven, my stepdaughter, apparently inherited her mother's keen eye and high standards for good writing. She read every word of the manuscript with care, saving me from a number of embarrassments and giving me some good ideas in the process. She also pointed out that I overuse the word *but,* perhaps because I am forever considering the other side of the case. So our private joke is that she helped me "kick *buts*" in this book. (But that joke is no longer private, I guess.)

Terry Chadsey, Marcy Jackson, and Rick Jackson are my close colleagues and dear friends at the Center for Courage & Renewal. For fifteen years, they have supported my work and helped "put wheels" on some of my ideas through the Center's superb programs. All of them read and commented on portions of this manuscript at various stages of its development, and Rick read several drafts from end to end, offering detailed responses to all of them. Because of you three, my life and work have been immeasurably enriched, and I am forever grateful.

In 2010, the Center for Courage & Renewal hosted two national conferences on democracy. My experience of leading and learning at both of them contributed mightily to this book. I am deeply grateful to all my friends on the Center's staff who helped make those events possible and to the people who attended for serving as an important community of discourse for me. Special thanks to my friends and colleagues Phillip Bimstein and Carrie Newcomer, musicians and citizens extraordinaire, who helped make those gatherings such compelling and memorable events.

Among the others with whom I discussed my manuscript or key ideas in it, special thanks to Dave Boyer, Kathy Gille, John Morefield, Kathy Morefield, Joan Philip, Jim Quay, Pamela Siegle, and Amey

Upton. All of them deepened my thinking and pointed me toward midcourse corrections that helped keep this book on track.

Finally (and here is a sentence I never imagined writing), I thank my conversation partners on Facebook. A couple of years ago, my friend Finn Ryan set up a Facebook author page for me. Grateful as I was, my skepticism about the medium kept me from posting anything there until six months before I finished this book. I am very glad that I took the leap. The folks who share that space with me have helped me refine a number of key ideas, allowing me to write a better book than I could have written alone. Many thanks to all my Facebook "friends" as well as my face-to-face friends.

[NOTES]

Epigraph

1. Terry Tempest Williams, "Engagement," *Orion*, July-Aug. 2004, http://www.orionmagazine.org/index.php/articles/article/143/. See also Williams, *The Open Space of Democracy* (Eugene, Ore.: Wip and Stock, 2004), pp. 83–84.

Prelude: The Politics of the Brokenhearted

1. Theodore Roethke, "In a Dark Time," in *The Collected Poems of Theodore Roethke* (New York: Anchor Books, 1974), p. 231.

2. Fifty percent of Americans "believe it is right for the government to monitor phone calls and e-mails, without court permission, to fight terrorism." *Atlantic*, Jan.-Feb. 2010, p. 56. See "Suspicious" at http://www.theatlantic.com/2010map

3. I first wrote about this in "The Politics of the Brokenhearted" in Mark Nepo, ed., *Deepening the American Dream* (San Francisco: Jossey-Bass, 2005).

4. Joshua Shenk, *Lincoln's Melancholy* (New York: Houghton Mifflin, 2005).

5. Matthew S. Holland, *Bonds of Affection* (Washington, D.C.: Georgetown University Press, 2007), p. 4.

6. For example, see Public Conversations Project, "A Model for an Introductory Dialogue on Abortion," 1999, http://www.publicconversations.org/node/62

7. Willynel, "George Carlin, Prophet," *Daily Kos,* May 22, 2010, http://www.dailykos.com/story/2010/5/22/868800/-George-Carlin, prophet

8. "About Us," *Soldier's Heart,* 2010, http://www.soldiersheart.net/about /index.shtml

9. Abraham Lincoln, "The Perpetuation of Our Political Institutions," speech delivered Jan. 27, 1838, http://www.teachingamericanhistory.org /library/index.asp?document=157. See also Ken Burns, "Commencement Address, 2006," speech delivered May 20, 2006, http://college.georgetown.edu/43685.html

Chapter I: Democracy's Ecosystem

1. E. M. Forster, *Two Cheers for Democracy* (New York: Harcourt, Brace, 1951), p. 70.

2. Molly Ivins, *You Got to Dance with Them What Brung You* (New York: Vintage Books, 1999), p. 81.

3. Robert D. Putnam, "*E Pluribus Unum:* Diversity and Community in the Twenty-First Century," *Journal of Scandinavian Political Studies,* 2007, *30,* 137–174, http://www.utoronto.ca/ethnicstudies/Putnam.pdf

4. Michael Jonas, "The Downside of Diversity," *New York Times,* Aug. 5, 2007, http://www.nytimes.com/2007/08/05/world/americas/05iht-diversity.1.6986248.html

5. Joshua Shenk, *Lincoln's Melancholy* (New York: Houghton Mifflin, 2005) p. 125.

6. Ibid.

7. Ibid.

8. See David Mathews, ". . . Afterthoughts," in *Kettering Review,* 2009, *27,* 68–69, for a similar list supported by some research findings.

9. Scott E. Page, *The Difference: How the Power of Diversity Creates Better Groups, Firms, Schools, and Societies* (Princeton, N.J.: Princeton University Press, 2008).

10. Bill Moyers, "Democracy Only Works When Ordinary People Claim It as Their Own," *Democracy NOW!* June 9, 2008, http://www.democracynow.org/2008/6/9/Moyers

11. David Gal and Derek D. Rucker, "When in Doubt, Shout! Paradoxical Influences of Doubt on Proselytizing," *Psychological*

Science, 2010, *21,* 1701–1707, doi: 10.1177/0956797610385953,
http://scipsy.files.wordpress.com/2010/10/psychological-science-2010-
gal-0956797610385953.pdf

12. "America's Founding Fathers," *Charters of Freedom,* n.d.,
http://www.archives.gov/exhibits/charters/constitution_
founding_fathers.html

13. Allegheny College, "Nastiness, Name-Calling, and Negativity: The
Allegheny College Survey of Civility and Compromise in American
Politics," Apr. 20, 2010, http://sitesmedia.s3.amazonaws.com/civility
/files/2010/04/AlleghenyCollegeCivilityReport2010.pdf, p. 3.

14. Ibid., p. 36.

15. Bill Moyers, *Moyers on Democracy* (New York: Anchor Books, 2009),
pp. 1–2.

16. Shenk, *Lincoln's Melancholy*, p. 8.

17. A "group decision-making process that seeks not only the agreement
of most participants but also the resolution or mitigation of
minority objections" whose aim is not just a decision but "group
solidarity." "Consensus Decision-Making," *Wikipedia,* Jan. 30, 2011,
http://en.wikipedia.org/wiki/Consensus_decision-making

18. See "Quaker Petition to Congress, October 4, 1783," *Charters
of Freedom,* http://www.archives.gov/exhibits/charters/charters_
of_freedom_zoom_pages/charters_of_freedom_zoom_5.1.1.html

19. "Underground Railroad," *Wikipedia,* Jan. 27, 2011, http://en
.wikipedia.org/wiki/Underground_Railroad

20. "Quaker Petition."

21. Gene Sharp, *Waging Nonviolent Struggle: 20th Century Practice and
21st Century Potential* (Manchester, N.H.: Extending Horizons Books,
2005).

22. For a detailed exploration of this point, see Paul Hawken, *Blessed Unrest*
(New York: Viking, 2007). See also Hawken's "World Index for Social
and Environmental Responsibility" (http://www.WiserEarth.org), "a
database of over 100,000 organizations in some 250 jurisdictions."
Barry Boyce, "Why We Need New Ways of Thinking," *Shambhala
Sun,* Sept. 2008, http://www.shambhalasun.com/index.php?option
=com_content&task=view&id=3246&Itemid=247

23. Howard Zinn, *You Can't Be Neutral on a Moving Train: A Personal History of Our Times* (Boston: Beacon Press, 2002), pp. 4–5.

24. See Bill Moyers, "For America's Sake," *Nation,* Jan. 22, 2007, http://www.thenation.com/article/americas-sake?page=0,3

25. Abraham Lincoln, "First Inaugural Address," Mar. 4, 1861, *Bartleby.com,* http://www.bartleby.com/124/pres31.html

Chapter II: Confessions of an Accidental Citizen

1. Leonard Cohen, "Democracy," on *The Future* (album), Nov. 1992. Lyrics copyright © 1992 Sony Music Entertainment (Canada)/ATV Music Publishing LLC.

2. Parker J. Palmer, *The Company of Strangers: Christians and the Renewal of America's Public Life* (New York: Crossroad, 1981).

3. William Sloane Coffin, *Credo* (Louisville, Ky.: Westminster/John Knox Press, 2005), p. 84.

4. See Angela D. Johnson, "In 2050, Half of U.S. Will Be People of Color," *DiversityInc,* Oct. 11, 2006, http://diversityinc.com/content /1757/article/311

5. Michelle Alexander, *The New Jim Crow: Mass Incarceration in the Age of Colorblindness* (New York: New Press, 2010). Quote is from "Legal Scholar Michelle Alexander on *The New Jim Crow: Mass Incarceration in the Age of Colorblindness*," *Democracy NOW!* Mar. 11, 2010, http://www.democracynow.org/2010/3/11 /legal_scholar_michelle_alexander_on_the

6. Joshua Shenk, *Lincoln's Melancholy* (New York: Houghton Mifflin, 2005), pp. 174–175.

7. Leo Damrosch, *Tocqueville's Discovery of America* (New York: Farrar, Straus and Giroux, 2010), p. 47.

8. Walt Whitman, *Leaves of Grass* (1900), http://www.bartleby.com/142/ 299.html

9. For further information, see "*Robert's Rules of Order,*" *Wikipedia,* http://en.wikipedia.org/wiki/Robert's_Rules_of_Order

10. I briefly summarized this teaching in Chapter VII of *The Courage to Teach,* where I mistakenly attributed it to the friend who made this visit

with me. He has since corrected me about who said what and when, and I am glad to amend the record.

11. Karen Armstrong, *The Case for God* (New York: Anchor Books, 2010), p. xvii.

12. See "Legal Scholar Michelle Alexander."

13. Alexis de Tocqueville, *Democracy in America,* trans. Arthur Goldhammer (New York: Library of America, 2004), p. 875.

14. Damrosch, *Tocqueville's Discovery,* pp. 107–108. Embedded quote from Tocqueville (Goldhammer), *Democracy in America.*

15. Alexis de Tocqueville, *Democracy in America,* trans. J. P. Mayer (New York: Anchor Books, 1969), p. 508.

16. Ibid.

17. Scott Briscoe, "De Tocqueville's America: Revisited," *Associations Now,* Sept. 2007, http://www.asaecenter.org/PublicationsResources /ANowDetail.cfm?ItemNumber=27937

18. Tocqueville (Goldhammer), *Democracy in America,* p. 598.

19. Alexis de Tocqueville, *Democracy in America*, Vol. 2, trans. Henry Reeve (Cambridge: Sever & Francis, 1863), pp. 132–133.

20. Robert Putnam's widely discussed *Bowling Alone* (New York: Simon & Schuster, 2000) depicts an America in which traditional forms of communalism have declined dramatically. But Putnam's subsequent book, *Better Together* (New York: Simon & Schuster, 2003), paints a more positive picture by examining emerging and alternative forms of associational life.

21. "In Hebrew, *chutzpah* is used indignantly, to describe someone who has overstepped the boundaries of accepted behavior with no shame. But in Yiddish and English, *chutzpah* has developed ambivalent and even positive connotations. *Chutzpah* can be used to express admiration for nonconformist but gutsy audacity." "Chutzpah," *Wikipedia,* Jan. 30, 2011, http://en.wikipedia.org/wiki/Chutzpah

22. The phrase "little platoons" is from Edmund Burke, *Reflections on the Revolution in France* (New York: Dover, 2006), p. 27.

23. Hafiz, "A Great Need," in *The Gift: Poems by Hafiz,* trans. Daniel Ladinsky (New York: Penguin Books, 1999), p. 165.

24. Whitman, *Leaves of Grass.*

Chapter III: The Heart of Politics

1. Terry Tempest Williams, "Engagement," *Orion*, July-Aug. 2004, http://www.orionmagazine.org/index.php/articles/article/143/

2. First statistic is from Richard Wilkinson and Kate Pickett, *The Spirit Level* (New York: Bloomsbury Press, 2009), p. v. Second is from G. William Domhoff, "Wealth, Income, and Power," *Who Rules America?* Jan. 2011, http://sociology.ucsc.edu/whorulesamerica/power/wealth.html. The comparison to 1928 is from Robert Reich, *Aftershock* (New York: Knopf, 2010), p. 6.

3. Leon Festinger, Henry W. Riecken, and Stanley Schachter, *When Prophecy Fails* (Minneapolis: University of Minnesota Press, 1956). See also David Gal and Derek D. Rucker, "When in Doubt, Shout! Paradoxical Influences of Doubt on Proselytizing," *Psychological Science,* 2010, *21,* 1701–1707, doi: 10.1177/0956797610385953, http://scipsy.files.wordpress.com/2010/10/psychological-science-2010-gal-0956797610385953.pdf, and "In Politics, Sometimes the Facts Don't Matter," *NPR,* July 13, 2010, http://www.npr.org/templates/story/story.php?storyId=128490874&ps=cprs

4. See "Charity: Who Cares?" *MintLife,* Dec. 10, 2009, http://www.mint.com/blog/trends/charity-who-cares/

5. Robert Borosage, "Greenspan: 'Shocked Disbelief,'" *Truthout,* Oct. 24, 2008, http://www.truth-out.org/102508C

6. Felix Salmon, "Greenspan's Apology: Still MIA," *Reuters,* Sept. 9, 2009, http://blogs.reuters.com/felix-salmon/2009/09/09/greenspans-apology-still-mia/

7. In what has been hailed by some as a breakthrough book, George A. Akerlof and Robert J. Shiller have argued for the prominent place emotional factors play in economic behavior. See their *Animal Spirits: How Human Psychology Drives the Economy and Why It Matters for Global Capitalism* (Princeton, N.J.: Princeton University Press, 2009).

8. Rachel Weiner, "Palin: Obama's 'Death Panels' Could Kill My Down Syndrome Baby," *Huffington Post,* Aug. 7, 2009, http://www.huffingtonpost.com/2009/08/07/palin-obamas-death-panel_n_254399.html

9. "St. Simeon the New Theologian" at "The Christian Origin of Heart Rhythm Mediation," *Institute for Applied Mediation,* 2009, http://www.appliedmeditation.org/About_IAM/christianity.shtml. See also Parker J. Palmer, *A Hidden Wholeness: The Journey Toward an Undivided Life* (San Francisco: Jossey-Bass, 2004).

10. Henry A. Giroux, "Living in a Culture of Cruelty: Democracy as Spectacle," Sept. 2, 2009, http://www.truth-out.org/090209R?n

11. See Matthew S. Holland, *Bonds of Affection* (Washington, D.C.: Georgetown University Press, 2007), pp. 1–17.

12. Jeffery Kaplan, "The Gospel of Consumption: And the Better Future We Left Behind," *Orion,* May-June 2008, p. 38, http://www.orionmagazine.org/index.php/articles/article/2962/

13. Don Peck, "How a New Jobless Era Will Transform America," *Atlantic,* Mar. 2010, http://www.theatlantic.com/doc/201003/jobless-america-future. The Friedman quote is from *The Moral Consequences of Economic Growth* (New York: Vintage Books, 2006), p. 3.

14. Jay Walljasper, "51 Ways to Spark a Commons Revolution," *Yes!* Oct. 21, 2010, http://www.yesmagazine.org/issues/a-resilient-community/51-ways-to-spark-a-commons-revolution

15. "Fascism," *Wikipedia,* Jan. 31, 2011, http://en.wikipedia.org/wiki/Fascism

Chapter IV: The Loom of Democracy

1. E. F. Schumacher, *Small Is Beautiful: Economics as If People Mattered* (New York: Harper & Row, 1973), pp. 97–98.

2. A loom is built "to hold the warp threads under tension to facilitate the interweaving of the weft threads." "Silk and Weaving," *World Threads,* 2005, http://worldthreads.com/boutique-wovens.htm

3. Abraham Lincoln, "Last Public Address," Apr. 11, 1865, *TeachingAmericanHistory.org,* http://teachingamericanhistory.org/library/index.asp?document=1099

4. Ibid.

5. Abraham Lincoln, "Last Public Address," Apr. 11, 1865, *Abraham Lincoln Online,* http://showcase.netins.net/web/creative/lincoln/speeches/last.htm

6. Schumacher, *Small Is Beautiful,* p. 103, emphasis added.

7. Joseph Ellis, *American Creation: Triumphs and Tragedies in the Founding of the Republic* (New York: Knopf, 2007), p. 123.

8. Ibid., pp. 90–91.

9. Lilly J. Goren, "Jefferson's Calm and Reason Now Thrown Off-Kilter," *Wisconsin State Journal,* July 2, 2010, p. A-10.

10. Ellis, *American Creation,* pp. 90–91, 123, 124, 125.

11. Ibid, p. 126.

12. See Michelle Alexander, *The New Jim Crow: Mass Incarceration in the Age of Colorblindness* (New York: New Press, 2010).

13. For a compelling example, see Bill Moyers's account of the dialogue on civil disobedience between President Lyndon Johnson and Martin Luther King Jr. in the weeks prior to the passage of that legislation: "Moyers on LBJ and MLK," *Bill Moyers Journal,* Jan. 18, 2008, http://www.pbs.org/moyers/journal/01182008/watch4.html

14. Daily Beast, "Washington's Homeless Power Brokers," *FORA.tv,* June 17, 2009, http://fora.tv/2009/06/17/Washingtons_Homeless_Power_Brokers; Tara Palmeri, "Homeless Stand In for Lobbyists on Capitol Hill," *CNNPolitics.com,* July 13, 2009, http://www.cnn.com/2009/POLITICS/07/13/line.standers/index.html

15. Carl Hulse, "In Books on Two Powerbrokers, Hints of the Future," *New York Times,* July 18, 2009, http://www.nytimes.com/2009/07/19/us/politics/19cong.html. On filibusters, see also Paul Krugman, "A Dangerous Dysfunction," *New York Times,* Dec. 20, 2009, http://www.nytimes.com/2009/12/21/opinion/21krugman.html?_r=1

16. The story is found in Amy Bach, *Ordinary Injustice: How America Holds Court* (New York: Metropolitan Books, 2009). The quotations come from the Booklist review of *Ordinary Injustice* found at http://www.ordinaryinjustice.com/reviews/reviews.html

17. Allen Tate, "Tension in Poetry," in *Essays of Four Decades* (Wilmington, Del.: Intercollegiate Studies Institute, 1999), p. 56.

18. "327: By Proxy," *WBEZ,* Mar. 9, 2007, http://www.thislife.org/radio-archives/episode/327/By-Proxy?bypass=true

19. David Crabtree, "Do the Liberal Arts Still Matter?" 2011, http://www.gutenberg.edu/pdfs/do_liberal_arts_still_matter.pdf

20. Abraham Lincoln, "First Inaugural Address," Mar. 4, 1861, *Bartleby.com*, http://www.bartleby.com/124/pres31.html

21. Shelley E. Taylor, *The Tending Instinct* (New York: Holt, 2003), p. 3.

22. Leo Damrosch, *Tocqueville's Discovery of America* (New York: Farrar, Straus and Giroux, 2010), p. 116.

23. Ibid., p. 117.

24. Ibid.

25. Ibid., pp. 117–118.

26. Alexis de Tocqueville, *Democracy in America*, Vol. 2 (New York: Quill Pen Classics, 2008), p. 245.

Chapter V: Life in the Company of Strangers

1. Rumi, "A Community of the Spirit," in *The Essential Rumi*, trans. Coleman Barks (San Francisco: HarperOne, 1997), p. 3.

2. I first told this story and wrote about this topic in my book *The Company of Strangers: Christians and the Renewal of America's Public Life* (New York: Crossroad, 1981). I am glad for a chance to revisit these themes, which seem no less timely today, and to remember my taxi driver. Although I had only one "class" with him, some thirty years ago, I still regard him as one of my great teachers.

3. Carissa Byrne Hessick, "Violence Between Lovers, Strangers, and Friends," *Washington University Law Review,* 2007, *85,* 344, http://lawreview.wustl.edu/inprint/85/2/Hessick.pdf

4. Alexis de Tocqueville, *Democracy in America*, Vol. 2 (New York: Quill Pen Classics, 2008), p. 245.

5. The ancient Greeks, like America's founders, also excluded women or slaves from participation in public life. This fact elicits dismay over the glacial pace of history when it comes to core issues of justice but also appreciation for certain achievements of American democracy over the past one hundred fifty years.

6. Ray Oldenburg, *The Great Good Place: Cafes, Coffee Shops, Bookstores, Bars, Hair Salons, and Other Hangouts at the Heart of a Community* (Saint Paul, Minn.: Paragon House, 1989).

7. Abraham Lincoln, "Address Before the Wisconsin State Agricultural Society," Sept. 30, 1859, http://showcase.netins.net/web/creative/lincoln/speeches/fair.htm; emphasis added.

8. Ibid., emphasis added.

9. Sara M. Evans and Harry C. Boyte, *Free Spaces: The Sources of Democratic Change in America* (Chicago: University of Chicago Press, 1992), p. 17.

10. Ibid., p. 18.

11. Dahlia Lithwick, "Why Can Shopping Malls Limit Free Speech?" *Slate,* Mar. 10, 2003, http://www.slate.com/id/2079885/

12. "Tea Party Movement," *New York Times,* Jan. 4, 2011, http://topics.nytimes.com/top/reference/timestopics/subjects/t/tea_party_movement/index.html

13. Ellen Tviet, "Tom's Drugstore: Building on the Energy of Campaign Season," Aug. 13, 2008, http://blog.lib.umn.edu/cdc/bythepeople/2008/08/toms_drugstore_building_on_the.php

14. See Brooke Jarvis, "Building the World We Want: Interview with Mark Lakeman," *Yes!* May 12, 2010, http://www.yesmagazine.org/happiness/building-the-world-we-want-interview-with-mark-lakeman?utm_source=aprmay10&utm_medium=email&utm_campaign=2_CityRhdr, and "The Vision of City Repair," *City Repair,* n.d., http://cityrepair.org/

15. Jarvis, "Building the World We Want."

16. Ibid.

17. Ibid.

18. Ibid.

19. See John McKnight and Peter Block, *The Abundant Community: Awakening the Power of Families and Neighborhoods* (San Francisco: Berrett-Koehler, 2010). See also the Abundant Community project Web site at http://www.abundantcommunity.com

20. "Crimes Against Property: Neighborhood Watch," *Law Library,* 2011, http://law.jrank.org/pages/11923/Crimes-Against-Property-Neighborhood-Watch.html

21. "Welcome to USAonWatch.org," *Neighborhood Watch Program/National Sheriffs' Association,* 2011, http://www.usaonwatch.org/. For rural examples, see "California Farmers Band Together via Farm Watch to Combat Agricultural Crime," *Neighborhood Watch News,* Dec. 14, 2009, http://www.usaonwatch.org/resource/ezine.aspx?EzineId=9. See also "Neighborhood Watch," *National*

Crime Prevention Council, 2011, http://www.ncpc.org/topics/home-and-neighborhood-safety/neighborhood-watch and ibid.

22. Hessick, "Violence."

23. Trevor Bennett, Katy Holloway, and David P. Farrington, *Does Neighborhood Watch Reduce Crime?* Washington, D.C.: U.S. Department of Justice Office of Community Oriented Policing Services, 2008, http://www.cops.usdoj.gov/files/RIC/Publications/e040825133-res-review3.pdf

24. "Neighborhood Association," *Wikipedia,* Jan. 12, 2011, http://en.wikipedia.org/wiki/Neighborhood_association

25. "Community Garden," *Wikipedia,* Jan. 25, 2011, http://en.wikipedia.org/wiki/Community_garden

26. "Seattle Department of Neighborhoods," *Seattle.gov,* 2011, http://www.cityofseattle.net/neighborhoods/

27. David Villano, "Building a Better Citizen," *Miller-McCune Magazine,* Nov.-Dec. 2009, p. 55, http://www.miller-mccune.com/politics/building-a-better-citizen-3361/

28. Ibid., p. 56. See also Jim Diers, *Neighborhood Power: Building Community the Seattle Way* (Seattle: University of Washington Press, 2004).

29. Villano, "Building a Better Citizen," p. 54.

30. Ibid.

31. C. Wright Mills, *The Sociological Imagination* (New York: Oxford University Press, 1959).

32. "Background and Statistics," *National Coalition for Homeless Veterans,* 2011, http://www.nchv.org/background.cfm

33. "Wendell Berry," *Wikipedia,* Feb. 4, 2011, http://en.wikipedia.org/wiki/Wendell_Berry

34. Wendell Berry, "The Art of the Commonplace," in *Sex, Economy, Freedom, and Community: Eight Essays* (New York: Pantheon, 1994), p. 173.

35. Wendell Berry, *Imagination in Place* (Berkeley, Calif.: Counterpoint, 2010), p. 32.

Chapter VI: Classrooms and Congregations

1. Walt Whitman, "Democratic Vistas," in *Whitman: Poetry and Prose,* ed. Justin Kaplan (New York: Library of America, 1996), p. 980.

2. Pew Forum on Religion and Public Life, "Frequency of Attendance at Religious Services by Religious Tradition," *U.S. Religious Landscape Survey,* Feb. 2008, http://religions.pewforum.org/pdf/table-frequency-of-attendance-at-religious-services-by-religious-tradition.pdf

3. Leo Damrosch, *Tocqueville's Discovery of America* (New York: Farrar, Straus and Giroux, 2010), p. 140.

4. Ibid., p. 50.

5. Ibid., p. 52.

6. Ibid., p. 116.

7. For a comprehensive study of this subject, see Robert D. Putnam and David E. Campbell, *American Grace: How Religion Divides and Unites Us* (New York: Simon & Schuster, 2010).

8. Jacob Needleman, "Two Dreams of America," in *Deepening the American Dream,* ed. Mark Nepo (San Francisco: Jossey-Bass, 2005), p. 25.

9. Hillel, *Pirke Avot* 1:14.

10. Rainer Maria Rilke, *Letters to a Young Poet,* trans. M. D. Herter (New York: Norton, 1993), p. 35.

11. I explore this and many other pedagogical possibilities in *The Courage to Teach: Exploring the Inner Landscape of a Teacher's Life* (San Francisco: Jossey-Bass, 1997 and 2007).

12. See Parker J. Palmer, "Foreword," in Joel Elkes, *Dr. Elkhanan Elkes of the Kovno Ghetto: A Son's Holocaust Memoir* (Orleans, Mass.: Paraclete Press, 1999).

13. Cited in Bill Moyers, *Healing and the Mind* (New York: Broadway Books, 2002), p. 174.

14. I pursue this theme in *The Courage to Teach;* this idea is also at the heart of the programs offered by the Center for Courage & Renewal (http://www.CourageRenewal.org).

15. See Parker J. Palmer "Evoking the Spirit in Public Education," *Educational Leadership*, Dec. 1998–Jan. 1999, http://www.couragerenewal.org/parker/writings/evoking-the-spirit

16. Kimberly E. Koehler Freitag, "Dead on Arrival: Democracy, Transcendence, and National Identity in the Age of *No Child Left Behind*," in *A Jeremiad on the Crisis of Democratic Civic Education,* ed. Kerry Burch. Thresholds in Education, vol. 34, no. 4. DeKalb, Ill.: Thresholds in Education Foundation, 2008.

17. Information about the Institute for Democratic Education in America can be found at http://www.democraticeducation.org/index.php. Another good source of ideas on this important topic is the Forum for Education and Democracy at http://forumforeducation.org/.

18. From personal correspondence with Scott Nine, used with his permission.

19. Also from Scott Nine's personal correspondence, used and edited with his permission:

> [Here are a few] on-the-ground things that educators seeking to foster democratic habits of the heart can immediately initiate: (1) Invite four or five students to a faculty meeting. (2) Ask students to facilitate important schoolwide meetings. (3) Ask students to develop rubrics for judging excellent work. (4) Allow students to read each other's papers and comment on them. (5) Allow students to decide what goes up on the walls at school. (6) Eat lunch with kids you rarely talk to and then listen generously. (7) Have students self-evaluate prior to parent-teacher conferences. (8) Ask teachers, principals, coaches, parents, school board members, administrators, and community leaders to take the standardized tests along with the students and report their scores right alongside the students' and openly discuss everyone's results together.

20. See National Service Learning Clearinghouse (http://www.servicelearning.org/), Campus Compact (http://www.campuscompact.org/), and National Youth Leadership Council (http://www.nylc.org/)

21. "Youth Civic Engagement," *Coalition for Youth,* 2011, http://www.hampton.gov/foryouth/youth_youth.html

22. David Villano, "Building a Better Citizen," *Miller-McCune Magazine,* Nov.-Dec. 2009, p. 53, http://www.miller-mccune.com/politics/building-a-better-citizen-3361. For a case study of the Hampton program, see Carmen Sirianni, *Investing in Democracy: Engaging Citizens in Collaborative Governance* (Washington, D.C.: Brookings Institution Press, 2009).

23. All quotations from Villano, "Building a Better Citizen," p. 57.

24. "Integrating Community Service and Classroom Instruction Enhances Learning: Results from an Experiment," *Educational Evaluation and Policy Analysis*, 1993, *15*, 410–419.

25. "Voters Say Election Full of Misleading and False Information," *World Public Opinion,* Dec. 9, 2010, http://www.worldpublicopinion.org /pipa/articles/brunitedstatescanadara/671.php?nid=&id=&pnt= 671&lb=

26. Mark Slouka, "Dehumanized: When Math and Science Rule the School," *Harper's,* Sept. 2009, pp. 36–37, http://www.harpers.org/ archive/2009/09/0082640

27. Thomas Jefferson, letter to W. C. Jarvis, Sept. 28, 1820, http://wist.info/jefferson-thomas/12694/

28. Anne Lamott, *Bird by Bird* (New York: Anchor Books, 1995), p. 22.

29. See Charter for Compassion (http://charterforcompassion.org/). See also Karen Armstrong, *The Case for God* (New York: Anchor Books, 2010), p. 45.

30. Michael Fuquay, "The Most Segregated Hour," *Beliefnet.com,* Jan. 2001, http://www.beliefnet.com/Entertainment/Books/2001/01/The-Most-Segregated-Hour.aspx

31. Tertullian, *Apology* 39:7, http://www.tertullian.org/anf/anf03/anf03-05.htm#P425_201743

32. See "Community Policing Defined," *Community Oriented Policing Services,* n.d., http://www.cops.usdoj.gov/default.asp?item=36

33. "Veteran-Civilian Dialogue," *Intersections,* 2010, http://www.intersectionsinternational.org/programs/consequences-conflict/veteran-civilian-dialogue, and Andrew Himes, "Veteran-Civilian Dialogue," Sept. 30, 2010, http://andrewhimes.net/content /veteran-civilian-dialogue

34. For more on decision making in the congregation, see Parker J. Palmer, *The Company of Strangers: Christians and the Renewal of America's Public Life* (New York: Crossroad, 1981). For more on counseling in the congregation, see Parker J. Palmer, *A Hidden Wholeness: The Journey Toward an Undivided Life* (San Francisco: Jossey-Bass, 2004).

35. The best book I know on the depths and details of this often misunderstood form of decision making is Michael J. Sheeran, *Beyond Majority*

Rule: Voteless Decisions in the Religious Society of Friends (Philadelphia: Yearly Meeting of the Religious Society of Friends, 1983).

36. A related approach is called Stephen Ministries (http://www.stephenministries.org/). I have no personal experience of this process, but people whom I trust recommend it.

37. Palmer, *Hidden Wholeness,* ch. 8. Many of the programs run by the Center for Courage & Renewal (http://www.CourageRenewal.org) offer an experiential education in this approach.

38. I was told this Hasidic tale by the philosopher Jacob Needleman, who kindly put it in writing for me so that I could recount it correctly.

39. Rainer Maria Rilke, *Letters to a Young Poet,* trans. Stephen Mitchell (New York: Vintage Books, 1986), pp. 88–89.

Chapter VII: Safe Space for Deep Democracy

1. Joseph Campbell (with Bill Moyers), *The Power of Myth* (New York: Anchor Books, 1991), p. 115.

2. Sara M. Evans and Harry C. Boyte, *Free Spaces: The Sources of Democratic Change in America* (Chicago: University of Chicago Press, 1992), pp. 17–18.

3. Leo Damrosch, *Tocqueville's Discovery of America* (New York: Farrar, Straus and Giroux, 2010), p. 116.

4. Terry Tempest Williams, "Engagement," *Orion,* July-Aug. 2004, http://www.orionmagazine.org/index.php/articles/article/143/

5. The quote is from William James, *The Principles of Psychology* (New York: Cosimo, 2007), p. 48.

6. "New National Poll Finds: More Americans Know Snow White's Dwarfs Than Supreme Court Judges, Homer Simpson Than Homer's *Odyssey,* and Harry Potter Than Tony Blair," *Zogby International,* Aug. 15, 2006, http://www.zogby.com/Soundbites/readclips.cfm?ID=13498

7. For a comprehensive 2010 survey of media habits and opinions among Americans, see "Americans Spending More Time Following the News," *Pew Research Center for the People and the Press,* Sept. 12, 2010, http://people-press.org/report/652/

8. Campbell, *Power of Myth,* p. 115.

9. Williams, "Engagement."

10. William Deresiewicz, "Solitude and Leadership," *American Scholar,* Spring 2010, http://www.theamericanscholar.org/solitude-and-leadership/

11. William H. Shannon, ed., *The Hidden Ground of Love* (New York: Farrar, Straus and Giroux, 1985), p. 455.

12. Ibid.

13. Thomas Merton, *Conjectures of a Guilty Bystander* (New York: Image/Doubleday, 1968), p. 86.

14. For more information, visit the Center's Web site at http://www .CourageRenewal.org

15. The capitalized phrase Circle of Trust, a registered trademark, is used to designate the programs offered by the Center for Courage & Renewal and facilitated by persons trained by the Center. The lowercase "circle of trust" refers to the process I wrote about in *A Hidden Wholeness: The Journey Toward an Undivided Life* (San Francisco: Jossey-Bass, 2004), which many people have adapted for their own use, often after experiencing one of the Center's programs. And yes, I am aware that in the movie *Meet the Parents,* Robert DiNiro's character refers to a "circle of trust" to great sardonic effect!

16. There is a body of literature on "workplace democracy" that takes a different slant on the relation of democracy and the workplace. Some resources on the topic can be found at the Web site for Workplace Change, http://www.colorado.edu/ibs/PEC/workplacechange /publications/democracy/

17. The Center for Courage & Renewal is not the only organization doing this kind of work, of course. See, for example, PeerSpirit (http://www.peerspirit.com/index.html) and the Institute for Circlework (http://www.instituteforcirclework.org/).

18. Emily Dickinson, "Poem 1129," *The Complete Poems of Emily Dickinson,* ed. Thomas H. Johnson (New York: Back Bay Books, 1976), p. 506.

19. Nelle Morton, *The Journey Is Home* (Boston: Beacon Press, 1985), pp. 55–56.

20. More details on these and other circle of trust principles and practices are available in *A Hidden Wholeness* and at "Foundations

of the Circle of Trust Approach," *Center for Courage & Renewal,* http://www.couragerenewal.org/about/foundations

21. Visit the Highlander Research and Education Center Web site at http://www.highlandercenter.org/; see also Myles Horton, *The Long Haul* (New York: Teachers College Press, 1997).

22. "Highlander Research and Education Center," *Wikipedia,* Feb. 6, 2011, http://en.wikipedia.org/wiki/Highlander_Folk_School

23. "History, 1953–1961: The Civil Rights Movement and the Citizenship Schools," *Highlander Research and Education Center,* n.d., http://www.highlandercenter.org/a-history2.asp

24. "Myles Horton and Highlander: 100 Years of Fighting for Justice," *Highlander Research and Education Center,* n.d., http://www.highlandercenter.org/pdf-files/horton-hrec-timeline-final02.pdf

25. David Schaper, " 'Camp Obama' Trains Campaign Volunteers," *NPR,* June 13, 2007, http://www.npr.org/templates/story/story.php?storyId= 11012254

26. Zack Exley, "Stories and Numbers: A Closer Look at Camp Obama," *Huffington Post,* Aug. 29, 2007, http://www.huffingtonpost.com/zack-exley/stories-and-numbers-a-clo_b_62278.html

27. Martin Sieff, "Obama, Dems Win Historic Blowout Victory," *UPI.com,* Nov. 5, 2008, http://www.upi.com/news/issueoftheday/2008/11/05/Obama-Dems-win-historic-blowout-victory/UPI-40391225895936/

28. Kelly Candaele and Peter Dreier, "The Year of the Organizer," *American Prospect,* Feb. 1, 2008, http://www.prospect.org/cs/articles?article= the_year_of_the_organizer

29. Marshall Ganz and Kate Hilton, "The New Generation of Organizers," *Shelter Force,* Feb. 12, 2010, http://www.shelterforce.org/article/print/ 1870/

30. Marshall Ganz, "What Is Public Narrative?" *New England Grassroots Environment Fund,* 2008, http://grassrootsfund.org/docs/ WhatIsPublicNarrative08.pdf

31. Hillel, *Pirke Avot* 1:14.

32. Marshall Ganz, "Why Stories Matter: The Art and Craft of Social Change," *Sojourners,* Mar. 2009, http://www.sojo.net/index

.cfm?action=magazine.article&issue=soj0903&article=why-
stories-matter; see also Ganz and Hilton, "New Generation of
Organizers."

33.   Ganz, "Why Stories Matter."

34.   Ibid.

35.   Exley, "Stories and Numbers."

36.   Ganz and Hilton, "New Generation of Organizers."

37.   "Cyberspace," *New Oxford American Dictionary*, 2nd ed. (New York:
Oxford University Press, 2005).

38.   Clay Shirkey, *Here Comes Everybody: The Power of Organizing Without
Organizations* (New York: Penguin, 2008).

39.   Malcolm Gladwell, "Small Change," *New Yorker,* Oct. 4,
2010, http://www.newyorker.com/reporting/2010/10/04
/101004fa_fact_gladwell?currentPage=all

40.   Ibid.

41.   Ibid.

42.   Evgeny Morozov, *The Net Delusion: The Dark Side of Internet Freedom*
(New York: Public Affairs, 2011).

43.   Roger Cohen, "Facebook and Arab Dignity," *New York Times,*
Jan. 24, 2011, http://www.nytimes.com/2011/01/25/opinion/25iht-
edcohen25.html?_r=1&hp

44.   A helpful annotated overview of various approaches to "e-democracy"
can be found at http://en.wikipedia.org/wiki/E-democracy. (Note that
the contents of this site are subject to change.)

45.   Tim Dickinson, "The Machinery of Hope," *Rolling Stone*, Mar. 20, 2008,
http://www.truth-out.org/article/rolling-stone-the-machinery-hope

Chapter VIII: The Unwritten History of the Heart

1.   Rainer Maria Rilke, "Turning Point," in *The Selected Poetry of Rainer
Maria Rilke,* trans. and ed. Stephen Mitchell (New York: Vintage
Books, 1982), pp. 134–135.

2.   John G. Neihardt, *Black Elk Speaks* (Albany: State University of New
York Press, 2008), pp. 2–4.

3.   Daniel J. Boorstein, *The Americans: The Democratic Experience* (New
York: Vintage Books, 1973), p. 532.

4.   Joseph Ellis, *American Creation: Triumphs and Tragedies in the Founding
of the Republic* (New York: Knopf, 2007), pp. 55–56.

5. Jeffrey M. Jones, "Americans See U.S. as Exceptional; 37% Doubt Obama Does," *Gallup,* Dec. 22, 2010, http://www.gallup.com

6. Joerg Wolf, "More Americans Believe That Saddam Was Directly Involved in 9/11," *Atlantic Review,* June 27, 2007, http://atlanticreview.org/archives/726-More-Americans-Believe-that-Saddam-Was-Directly-Involved-in-911.html

7. Christopher Hellman and Travis Sharp, "The FY 2009 Pentagon Spending Request: Global Military Spending," *Center for Arms Control and Non-Proliferation,* Feb. 22, 2008, http://armscontrolcenter.org/policy/securityspending/articles/fy09_dod_request_global/

8. Dan Froomkin, "Social Immobility: Climbing the Economic Ladder Is Harder in the U.S. Than in Most European Countries," *Huffington Post,* Mar. 17, 2010, http://www.huffingtonpost.com/2010/03/17/social-immobility-climbin_n_501788.html; "A Family Affair: Intergenerational Social Mobility Across OECD Countries," *Economic Policy Reforms: Going for Growth* (Paris: Organization for Economic Cooperation and Development, 2010), http://www.oecd.org/dataoecd/2/7/45002641.pdf

9. Pew Social Trends Staff, "Inside the Middle Class: Bad Times Hit the Good Life," *Pew Research Center,* "Social and Demographic Trends," Apr. 9, 2008, http://pewsocialtrends.org/2008/04/09/inside-the-middle-class-bad-times-hit-the-good-life/

10. Sonia Sotomayor, "A Latina Judge's Voice," speech delivered Oct. 26, 2001, at the University of California, Berkeley, http://berkeley.edu/news/media/releases/2009/05/26_sotomayor.shtml

11. In article 1, section 2, paragraph 3 of the U.S. Constitution, slaves are counted as three-fifths of a person for the purposes of distributing tax revenues and apportioning members of Congress.

12. On Rosa Parks's prior history of involvement in justice and social change issues, see Danielle L. McGuire, *At the Dark End of the Street* (New York: Knopf, 2010).

13. John Meachum, "Trust and Caution," review of *American Creation* by Joseph J. Ellis, *New York Times,* Nov. 11, 2007, http://www.nytimes.com/2007/11/11/books/review/Meacham-t.html

14. Reinhold Niebuhr, *The Irony of American History* (Chicago: University of Chicago Press, 2008), p. 63.

[THE AUTHOR]

P arker J. Palmer is a writer, teacher, and activist whose work speaks deeply to people in many walks of life. Author of nine books—including the best sellers *The Courage to Teach, Let Your Life Speak,* and *A Hidden Wholeness*—his writing has been recognized with ten honorary doctorates and numerous national awards, including the 2010 William Rainey Harper Award (previously won by Margaret Mead, Marshall McLuhan, Paulo Freire, and Elie Wiesel). In 2005, Jossey-Bass published *Living the Questions: Essays Inspired by the Work and Life of Parker J. Palmer,* written by notable practitioners in a variety of fields, including medicine, law, philanthropy, politics, economic development, and K–12 and higher education. He is founder and senior partner of the Center for Courage & Renewal and holds a Ph.D. from the University of California at Berkeley.

[INDEX]

service, 131–132; students having a
voice in their own, 130, 140; and
teaching, done well, 127–128. *See
also* Education
Leisure time, lack of, 105
Letters to a Young Poet (Rilke), 124
Lewis, J., 164
Liberal education, 84, 150
Liberation movements, 184
Libraries, public, 105, 107
Lies. *See* Falsehoods
Limiting space, 152
Lincoln, A., 3–4, 6, 8–9, 10n, 13–14,
15, 19, 26–27, 35, 61, 69, 70–71,
84–85, 95–96, 98
Lincoln's Melancholy (Shenk),
3–4
Listening, importance of, 5, 160,
161, 162
Literary scholars, 125
Lobbyists, actions of, 79
Love: and heartbreak, 57, 60; power of,
69, 71; saved by, 193
Lower class. *See* Poverty
Luke 24, 148

M

Madison, J., 155, 192
Mailboxes, 111
Majority rule, issue of, 20, 21, 144
Mandela, N., 185, 188
Marketplace of ideas, 12
Marty, M., 156
Mass media, 25, 33, 58, 152–155
Math education, 134
McCarthyism, 2
McDonald's, 106
Meachum, J., 192
Meaning, search for. *See* Inner search
Media, the. *See* Mass media
Medieval curriculum, 84
Melting pot myth, 182–183
Mental dismissal of others, 127

Merton, T., 156–158
Metaphors, use of, 160, 183
Middle class, the, 2, 51, 93, 182, 183
Mills, C. W., 115
Money magazine, 132
Montgomery bus boycott, 164, 185
*Moral Consequences of Economic Growth,
The* (Friedman), 64
Morozov, E., 171
Mortality, 1, 2, 83, 175, 189
Movie theaters, 105, 107, 108
Moyers, B., 16, 18–19
Mubarak regime, 171
Muhammad, Prophet, 148n
Multiple-use spaces, 108
Museums, 100–101, 105
Music, 160
Myanmar, 185
Myths: maintaining the pretense of,
issue with, 181; national, American,
178–180; nature of, 177; qualifying,
issue with, 180; rightly understood,
meaning of, 176–178; today's
national, versions of, 182–183;
various interpretations of,
176

N

Narcissism, collective, 187–188
National anthem, 180
National Association for the
Advancement of Colored People
(NAACP), 185
National pride, 183
Nationalism, diseased brand of, 65
Native Americans, 34
Nazism, 65, 76, 152
Needleman, J., 122
Negative stress, 13
Neglected infrastructure, 9–10
Neighborhood associations, 112
Neighborhood watch programs,
111–112

This constitutes a continuation of the copyright page:

Chapter II: Democracy's Ecosystem
"Democracy" by Leonard Cohen from *The Future*. © 1992 Sony/ATV Music Publishing LLC. All rights administered by Sony/ATV Music Publishing LLC, 8 Music Square West, Nashville, TN 37203. All rights reserved. Used by permission.
Excerpts from Leo Damrosch, *Tocqueville's Discovery of America*. Copyright © 2010 by Leo Damrosch. Published by Farrar, Straus & Giroux. (Note: Excerpts also appear in Chapters IV and VI.)
"A Great Need" from the Penguin publication *The Gift: Poems by Hafiz*, translated by Daniel Ladinsky. Copyright © 1999 Daniel Ladinsky and used with his permission.

Chapter V: Life in the Company of Strangers
"A Community of the Spirit" from the HarperCollins book *The Essential Rumi*, translations by Coleman Barks with John Moyne. Copyright © 1995 by Coleman Barks and reprinted with his permission.
"Building the World We Want: Interview with Mark Lakeman" by Brooke Jarvis in *YES! Magazine*, May 12, 2010. Reprinted with permission.
"Building a Better Citizen" by David Villano in *Miller-McCune Magazine*, November/December 2009. Reprinted by permission of the author and Miller-McCune Magazine.

Chapter VI: Classrooms and Congregations
"Dead on Arrival: Democracy, Transcendence, and National Identity in the Age of No Child Left Behind" by Kimberly E. Koehler in *Democracy in Education* (Dekalb, IL: Thresholds in Education, 2008). Reprinted with permission.
"Dehumanized: When Math and Science Rule the School" by Mark Slouka from *Essays In the Nick of Time* (Graywolf Press), as originally published in *Harper's Magazine*, September 2009. Reprinted with permission.

Chapter VII: Safe Space for Deep Democracy
"Stories and Numbers—a Closer Look at Camp Obama" by Zack Exley in *The Huffington Post*, August 29, 2007.
"Why Stories Matter: The Art and Craft of Social Change" by Marshall Ganz is reprinted with permission from *Sojourners*, March 2009. (800) 714–7474, www.sojo.net.
"Small Change: Why the Revolution Will Not Be Tweeted" by Malcolm Gladwell in *The New Yorker*, October 4, 2010. Reprinted by permission of the author.

Chapter VIII: The Unwritten History of the Heart
Excerpt from "Turning-Point" in *The Selected Poetry of Rainer Maria Rilke*, by Rainer Maria Rilke, translated by Stephen Mitchell. Copyright © 1982 by Stephen Mitchell. Used by permission of Random House, Inc. and Stephen Mitchell.
"Trust and Caution" by Jon Meacham from *The New York Times Sunday Book Review*, November 11, 2007. Copyright © 2007 The New York Times. All rights reserved. Reprinted with permission.

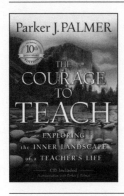

The Courage to Teach:
Exploring the Inner Landscape
of a Teacher's Life

10th Anniversary Edition

Parker J. Palmer

Hardcover/CD
ISBN: 978-0-7879-9686-4

"This book is for teachers who have good days and bad—and whose bad days bring the suffering that comes only from something one loves. It is for teachers who refuse to harden their hearts, because they love learners, learning, and the teaching life."—From the Introduction

In the tenth anniversary edition of his classic *The Courage to Teach*, Parker J. Palmer offers hope, encouragement, and guidance to teachers—and other professionals—who want to recover the heart of their vocation and calling. His new Foreword reflects on ten years of "courage work," which has spread beyond education to help teachers and other professionals recover meaning and depth in their work lives. And a new concluding chapter takes a fresh look at a new kind of professional and what it means to "take heart" in one's work.

BONUS: Includes an audio CD featuring a 45-minute conversation between Parker Palmer and his colleagues Marcy Jackson and Estrus Tucker from the Center for Courage & Renewal (www.CourageRenewal.org). They reflect on what they have learned from working with thousands of teachers in their "Courage to Teach" program and with others who yearn for greater integrity in their professional lives.

Let Your Life Speak:
Listening for the Voice of Vocation

Parker J. Palmer

Paper
ISBN: 978-0-470-58063-9

"Parker Palmer's writing is like a high country stream-clear, vital, honest. If your life seems to be passing you by, or you cannot see the way ahead, immerse yourself in the wisdom of these pages and allow it to carry you toward a more attentive relationship with your deeper, truer self."—**John S. Mogabgab**, editor, *Weavings* journal

"An exuberant and passionate book. I was deeply moved and I cannot, nor do I want to, shake off the haunting questions that it raises for me. This book penetrates the soul, and it will definitely stir you to explore more of your own inner territory. What an extraordinary achievement."—**Jim Kouzes**, coauthor, *The Leadership Challenge* and *Encouraging the Heart*; chairman, Tom Peters Group/Learning Systems

In this honest and compelling meditation, Parker Palmer reflects upon vocation, spirit, and the life journey with a depth of insight that will touch anyone who yearns for an authentic way of standing and serving in the world. Finding one's calling is not just about finding something we can do—it is about finding what we can't not do. "Let your life speak" is a time-honored Quaker admonition to live one's life as witness to the deepest truths one knows. But as Parker Palmer explains, those words can also mean "Listen to your life and let it tell you what your truth is." Vocation, he writes, comes not from external demands but from listening to "true self"—a listening that will always call us into some form of service to others. Though the details of his journey are singular, he draws from it that which is universal. The result is a moving and illuminating book for anyone who seeks not just a job but a calling—and companionship along the way.

A Hidden Wholeness:
The Journey Toward an Undivided Life

Parker J. Palmer

Hardcover
ISBN: 978-0-7879-7100-7

A BookSense Pick, September 2004

"This book is a treasure—an inspiring, useful blueprint for building safe places where people can commit to 'act in every situation in ways that honor the soul.'"—*Publishers Weekly*

"The soul is generous: it takes in the needs of the world. The soul is wise: it suffers without shutting down. The soul is hopeful: it engages the world in ways that keep opening our hearts. The soul is creative: it finds its way between realities that might defeat us and fantasies that are mere escapes. All we need to do is to bring down the wall that separates us from our own souls and deprives the world of the soul's regenerative powers."—**From** *A Hidden Wholeness*

In *A Hidden Wholeness*, Parker J. Palmer reveals the same compassionate intelligence and informed heart that shaped his bestselling books, *Let Your Life Speak* and *The Courage to Teach*. Here he speaks to our yearning to live undivided lives–in a world filled with the forces of fragmentation. *A Hidden Wholeness* weaves together four themes: the shape of an integral life, the meaning of community, teaching and learning for transformation, and nonviolent social change.

Defining a "circle of trust" as "a space between us that honors the soul," Palmer shows how people in settings ranging from friendship to organizational life can support each other on the journey toward living "divided no more." The hundreds of thousands of people who know Parker J. Palmer's books will be glad to find the journey continued here—and readers new to his work will be glad they joined that journey.

Interested in exploring and experiencing more?

Parker Palmer founded the Center for Courage & Renewal to "put wheels" on the ideas in his books, including this one. We have worked closely for many years, developing and offering retreats, programs, and resources aimed at cultivating the "habits of the heart" that lead to more authentic, meaningful, and engaged lives.

Please visit our website to learn more about opportunities:

- to reflect and replenish yourself,
- to concentrate on what matters,
- to connect with others seeking similar insights, and
- to bring greater possibilities to your personal, professional, and civic life.

www.CourageRenewal.org